Second Edition

AMERICAN GOVERNMENT
As It Truly Is

Ishmael Tarikh

De Anza College
Foothill College

Kendall Hunt
publishing company

Cover image © Shutterstock, Inc.

Kendall Hunt
publishing company

www.kendallhunt.com
Send all inquiries to:
4050 Westmark Drive
Dubuque, IA 52004-1840

Printed in the United States of America
10 9 8 7 6 5 4 3 2 1

For my grandfather, Henry Edward Winckler, and the next generation of Tarikhs: Aziza, Askia, Jaylen, Jailah, and Amina

CONTENTS

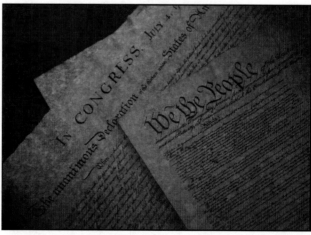

Image © Stephen Coburn, 2009. Used under license from Shutterstock, Inc.

PREFACE

There are but a handful of people who can honestly say that there is nothing in this life that speaks to their passion. I have been fortunate enough to have several passions. Among these, and high on the list, is politics. Over the last thirty-plus years I have pursued my passion for politics in many ways. Academically, I have made the pursuit through the disciplines of political science, ethnic studies, sociology, and law. I first began to instruct American government classes at Berkeley (CA) High School in the early 1990s. Since that time I have taught political science courses to community college students and undergraduates at several California postsecondary institutions.

American education has changed in significant ways over the aforementioned period of time. Generally, students are less academically prepared than those of a mere generation or two ago. Students are also less likely to understand or appreciate an integrated approach to their formal education. In my classes I conduct a straw poll every academic term that asks how many students are enrolled due to their enthusiasm for learning more about our government. The consistent outcome is that fewer than one out

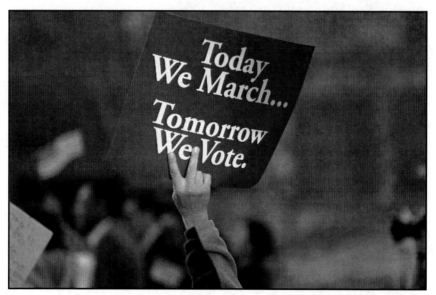

Image © Jorge Salcedo, 2009. Used under license from Shutterstock, Inc.

of ten of my students respond in the affirmative. The reality is that the overwhelming majority of my students take the basic course in American government because it fulfills a General Education requirement. There are growing numbers of these students who exhibit some level of hostility toward being required to learn more about their government.

The consequence is that there is an inherent friction between the students' objectives and my objectives for the course. I want them to accumulate knowledge about the subject matter in order to be empowered. They want good grades. It is my hope that this *American Government: As It Truly Is* can bridge the gap between the objectives.

The purpose of this book is to provide some context to the other required readings in any basic American government course. It has been written to be useful to high school, college, and university students. This book should make available to students a perspective about our government that not only challenges the status quo, but that also challenges the manner in which the status quo was achieved. This work is largely about encouraging young Americans to play a more active and participatory role in the functioning of our government. Although efforts to increase the voting turnout of youth in America are important, voting alone will not make the goals of the Preamble to the Constitution a reality for as many Americans as is humanly possible. Another purpose of this book is to emphasize the necessity of taking action on the many days that precede and follow the first Tuesday in November in even-numbered calendar years.

The structure of the book is a bit of intellectual masonry. We begin with what is most important: the history of the development of the American body politic. Accordingly, the first two chapters are the foundation of the edifice. The third chapter takes the basic governance concepts from abstractions to actual structure. Chapters four, five, and six mirror the three branches of our national government. Chapter seven attempts to place a capstone on the building by suggesting some approaches that could reshuffle the deck in anticipation of a more equitable outcome.

I have also included a study guide after each chapter. The Study Guides for Chapters 1, 2, 3, and 6 are self explanatory. Matters relating to Interest Groups can be found in the Chapter 4 Study Guide. Matters relating to Foreign Policy can be found in the Chapter 5 Study Guide. Matters relating to current events can be found in the Chapter 7 Study Guide. The study guide at the very end (after Chapter 7) is entitled "For Your Consideration . . . California State Matters."

I have included a table of cases and a subject-name index for quick reference purposes.

I do not expect anything like agreement about the suggestions, but they are excellent conversation starters. The time is ripe for Americans to consider changing the relationship between government and its citizens. The events of the past seven years should provide us the motivation to realize that Americans and the American government have serious adjustments to make in order to remain fluid in a world that is dynamically changing.

This effort would not have been possible without a host of supporters. I must first thank my mother, B. W. Wyatt, for the many evenings that she personally escorted my siblings and I to the local public library after long days on a stressful job. Throughout my formative years, my mother made it clear that anything less than stellar academic achievement was not tolerable, and that developing critical thinking skills was more important than earning high grades. I must also thank my siblings Nancy, Edwyna, and Odie for nurturing Baby Brother. As a child of the 1960s, I can attest that the quality of public ghetto schooling in California surpassed the quality of much of today's schooling (public or private), with its anti-intellectual, test-driven robotism.

Second, much gratitude is due to my intellectual sounding board, Dr. Kamau Kemayo of the University of Illinois, Springfield. He and I have nourished each other since meeting in graduate school at UCLA over twenty-five years ago. Many thanks are in order for Dr. Halford Fairchild and Dr. Melvin Oliver. Also, my thanks go to my numerous colleagues over the years at Berkeley High School, Chico State University, UC, Santa Cruz, De Anza College, and San Jose State University.

Last, there could not be enough said of my brothers of Upsilon Chapter of Kappa Alpha Psi Fraternity, Inc. Their unswerving fidelity has brought us all from being struggling young men to becoming the leaders of a generation. When I am in their presence I am dwarfed by the enormity of their achievements. To them I unequivocally state: I remain yours in the bond.

Questions, suggestions, and comments about the book are welcomed via e-mail: tarikhishmael@fhda.edu.

I. Tarikh
August 2013
Cupertino, California

CHAPTER 1

The Historical and Philosophical Roots of the American Republic

Image © Marek Slusarcyzk, 2009. Used under license from Shutterstock, Inc.

Foundations of the Republic

Most American government textbooks provide a cursory background of the British roots of the founding of this republic. Here, a more thorough treatment of those roots is provided for two reasons. First, because a deeper awareness of the foundational thinking will provide a greater understanding of the motivations of the founders. Second, because it is crucial to resist the current American approach of devaluing the history and the attendant inability to make necessary linkages between yesterday, today, and tomorrow.

Magna Carta

Thus, a document that can be viewed in its original form at the National Archives in Washington, D.C., is our starting point. That document is the

Magna Carta, which was published in 1215. This was the first document that placed limits on the British monarchy. It is also where the first mention of the Great Writ of Habeas Corpus can be found. This extraordinary writ was deemed so important by the founders, that narrow limits on it can be found in Article I, Section 9 of the United States Constitution. Moreover, in recent years, in matters relating to the War on Terror, the United States Supreme Court has repeatedly reaffirmed our adherence to the near 800-year tradition that a person deprived of her or his liberty is entitled to a hearing before a magistrate.

Limits on the Monarchy

The notion that limits could be placed on the British monarchy were by no means resolved in the 13th Century, though. There were two competing schools of thought on the matter. One school asserted that absolute authority was to be enjoyed by the Crown. The other asserted that only relative authority was to be enjoyed by the Crown. In the former, the two personalities of note are Thomas Hobbes, and Sir Robert Filmer. In the latter, the two personalities are John Locke, and Jean-Jacques Rousseau. Although Rousseau was a Frenchman and not a Briton, his influence on historical figures such as Alexis de Tocqueville and Thomas Jefferson is undeniable.

Social Contract Tradition

Thomas Hobbes (1588–1679) is credited with being the founder of what has become known as the Social Contract Tradition. In 1651 he published *Leviathan,* which supported absolutism and rejected the concept of a separation of powers. For Hobbes, all legitimate authority rested squarely in the Crown. He believed that the sovereign power was not a party to the social contract, and it therefore was not bound by it. According to Hobbes, the state of nature was asocial and apolitical. This rejection of the Aristotelian claim that man is by nature a political animal was arguably an unusual twist for a Western political philosopher. He also posited that the motivation to cede individual rights to the sovereign was for pragmatic self-interest. But, in Hobbes's defense, his way of thinking predates the Age of Enlightenment. The time when reason was considered the primary source and legitimacy for authority would not come until a decade after his death. For the purposes of this text, the Age of Enlightenment is considered to have begun with the Glorious Revolution of 1688, and ended with the

French Revolution of 1789. Hence, colloquially put, Hobbes got the party started, but didn't hang around for the uncorking of the champagne.

Sir Robert Filmer (1588–1653) based the absolute authority of kings on the authority given to Adam by God to rule the family. His most famous work, *Patriarcha*, was posthumously published in 1680. It was written as a defense of the divine right of kings to rule. It is most noteworthy because it is also the basis for the refutation of absolutism found in John Locke's First *Treatise of Government*. In Filmer's lifetime, Britain was bedeviled by a series of English Civil Wars that lasted from 1642 to 1651. The very nature of authority was being fought over between Royalists, dubbed *Cavaliers*, and Parliamentarians, dubbed *Roundheads*.

The victory of the Roundheads under the leadership of Oliver Cromwell is significant to American history. This is because the Roundheads were Puritans, and Cromwell's abolishing the British monarchy and taking the unique title of Lord Protector of the Commonwealth (1653–1658) left sore wounds. The Puritan undermining of the monarchy sets the stage for the abusive treatment that the eventual Puritan settlers in North America had to endure while they were still in Europe. The backlash against the Roundheads was so strong that Cromwell's body was exhumed, ghoulishly hung in chains, and beheaded, upon the return to power of the Royalists in 1660. The body remained on display for 25 years.

The Glorious Revolution

The Glorious Revolution of 1688 is related to the American Revolution because limits were once again placed on the British monarchy. Two converging dilemmas greeted King James II of England (James VII of Scotland). In the first place, he had big problems because he was Catholic, and he was viewed as too close to France's Louis XIV. This was particularly problematic because of the close association with the Catholic King and his belief in the divine right of kings to rule absolutely. This political dominance of white Anglo Saxon Protestants (WASPs) remains evident today. If this does not sound credible, review the widespread distrust of the presidential candidacy of John Fitzgerald Kennedy in 1960, the subtle inferences about John Kerry's presidential candidacy in 2004, and the not-so-subtle inferences about the Mormon beliefs of Mitt Romney during his presidential candidacy in 2008.

In the second place, King James's reign became embroiled in the still simmering aftermath of the English Civil Wars. As mentioned, this was the battle between the divine right of the Crown, and the political rights of Parliament. The so-called bloodless revolution resulted in Protestant William of Orange and his wife Mary II ascending to the British throne. However, in order to end the revolution, William and Mary agreed to the English Bill of Rights in 1689, which was an Act of Parliament. That Bill of Rights is quite similar to the first eight amendments to the United States Constitution. They also agreed to a constitutional monarchy, and they extinguished the thought that there would ever again be a Catholic monarchy in England.

The political dominance of WASPs has existed in England and America ever since. Although the battleground for religious differences now manifests most obviously over Northern Ireland, America's modern contribution is cyclically displayed. If this does not sound credible, review the widespread and ongoing distrust of the Obama presidency. The Reverend Jeremiah Wright debacle revealed the major adjustment necessary to accept a chief executive who does not fit the mainstream conception of any previous president of the United States.

Natural Rights

John Locke (1632–1704) is one of the most important Western political philosophers. His brand of liberalism is the very foundation of our system of government. While in exile during the tumult of the Glorious Revolution in 1689, he penned his most famous work, *Two Treatises of Government*. Upon his return to England after the revolution, he espoused the idea that human nature is based on reason and tolerance. He, like Hobbes, subscribed to social contract theory. But, unlike Hobbes, he called for a separation of powers, considered the sovereign to be a party to the social contract, and believed in the right of citizens to revolt. Locke's *Second Treatise on Government* outlined what government should be, and why men submit to the authority of the state. According to Locke, the basis of authority, and its legitimacy, is the consent of the governed. Civil society was created for the protection of property, and the rights of man are natural. This means they are bestowed by God, and they cannot be taken away by man. However, men can voluntarily submit to authority, as long as the duty the state has to protect remains fulfilled.

Jean-Jacques Rousseau (1712–1778) published *The Social Contract* in 1762. Unlike Hobbes, he believed the basis of popular sovereignty is the general will of the people, not the divine right of kings. Unlike Locke, he rejected representative democracy. Rousseau believed in the superiority of direct democracy, because it would yield a collective interest. It is a fair statement to characterize American ideology as a hybrid of the Social Contract outlooks of Hobbes and Locke. Rousseau's collective interest and direct democracy have been largely rejected. Thomas Jefferson's following of Locke's natural rights, which encompass property rights, is clearly evident in the language of the Declaration of Independence. Had Jefferson followed the collective interest dictates of Rousseau, Locke's "life, liberty, and the pursuit of property" would likely have been changed to "life, liberty, and the pursuit of social justice," instead of "life, liberty, and the pursuit of happiness."

Linkage to Today

The Obama Administration is today grappling with accusations of socialism because it has shifted the emphasis of the social contract from Locke to a more Rousseau-like approach. Though Locke's approach to the social contract left the necessary theoretical flexibility to allow the institution of slavery and the slave trade, Rousseau's approach did not. At the core of the difference is the focus on what is good for the individual, as opposed to what is good for society as a whole. The resiliency of the ownership/ property approach is under the greatest strain in recent memory due to the current collapse of the financial structure. As the foundation for the creation of the American body politic continues to be laid, this dilemma of me versus we will repeatedly resurface.

Chapter 1
Study Guide

1. In lecture, what has been called the "Great Writ" [dating back almost 800 years]?

   a: rigor mortis   c: coitus interruptus
   b: stare decisis   d: habeas corpus

2. A set of beliefs that includes a limited role for the national government in helping individuals, support for traditional values and lifestyles, and a cautious response to change is called _____.

   a: capitalism   c: fascism
   b: conservatism   d: liberalism

3. To ensure that majority rule does not become oppressive, modern democracies:

   a: have constitutions that are difficult to amend
   b: hold free, competitive elections
   c: provide guarantees of minority rights
   d: use plurality voting for most decisions

4. One of the revolutionary ideas of John Locke was the idea that people have:

   a: a right to a secure job
   b: a right to welfare if they need it
   c: natural rights
   d: a right to adequate health care
   e: a right to checks and balances in government

5. Pluralist theory asserts that decisions are made in American politics by:

   a: the competition between groups trying to gain benefits for their members
   b: the mass population
   c: the governing elites
   d: the wealthy

6. Which of the following *was not* a concept within John Locke's political philosophy?

   a: life, liberty, and the pursuit of property
   b: consent of the governed
   c: natural rights of man
   d: life, liberty, and the pursuit of happiness

7. If you are either skeptical of, or oppose, almost all government activities on the traditional political spectrum you would be labeled a:

   a: socialist   d: libertarian
   b: liberal   e: communist
   c: conservative

8. In this type of regime the government is fully controlled by the ruler, but not all social and economic institutions:

   a: totalitarian   d: democratic
   b: authoritarian   e: theocratic *religious*
   c: libertarian

9. Identify the correct chronological order of economic systems:

   a: capitalism/barbarism/colonialism
   b: theocracy/aristocracy/democracy
   c: monarchy/aristocracy/democracy
   d: feudalism/mercantilism/colonialism/capitalism
   e: none of the above

10. The Glorious Revolution (1688) created the political dominance of this group in England, and in America:

   a: Republicans   d: Whigs
   b: Democrats   e: Tories
   c: WASPs

11. All of the following are included in theories on Classical Liberalism except:

   a: it is hegemonistic
   b: it is optimistic
   c: it favors the individual over the group
   d: it supports free-market economics
   e: it places reason before faith

12. All of the following are included in theories on Classical Republicanism except:
    a: it is concerned with property
    b: it believes in the authority of people, but seeks to keep them at a distance from power
    c: it believes in a separation of powers
    d: it believes in protecting the rights of individuals
    e: it places faith before reason

13. Identify the author and text that set the foundation for the profit driven economic system of capitalism:
    a: Adam Smith/Wealth of Nations
    b: John Locke/Two Treatises of Government
    c: Rousseau/The Social Contract
    d: Karl Marx/Das Capital

CHAPTER 2

From Colonies
to Confederation

Image © Kenneth V. Pilon, 2009. Used under license from Shutterstock, Inc.

Colonial America

Perhaps it is now clear that this treatment of the American government is not going to be devoid of history. Arguably, the absence of historical analyses has created cycles of repetition for our government and its citizens that are neither natural, nor unavoidable. It is important to consider that the aforementioned philosophical developments that lent their substance to the creation of the American body politic did not occur in a vacuum. As far as economic systems are concerned, their development on the world stage is informative to understanding the competing interests that dominated, and that continue to greatly affect our government and its approaches and policies.

Feudalism

Feudalism is the first economic system of note, because it predates the proceeding two. The feudalism of Europe created an aristocracy that has changed in its manifestations over time, but that continues in its motivations. The same hierarchical relationship that existed between feudal lord and serf under feudalism also existed between mother country and colony under mercantilism, and between owners and workers under capitalism. In feudalism, the serf was bound to produce from the land for life. In colonialism, the slave was bound to produce from the land for life. In capitalism, the worker is bound to produce, but the tie to the land has been displaced. At first, this displacement was with the factory, but now it is with the computer. For many, there are distinctions among these economic systems, but there is little difference in terms of the plight of those who are farthest away from the ownership class.

Feudalism was an economic system that rested on the exploitation of the labor power of agricultural workers. It was a system in which there was the extraction of goods from the land, which were taken to the marketplace to be bartered or sold as commodities. The glue that held feudalism together was the use of intimidation and force against the serfs. This force was usually meted out by the nobles, who gained their position by virtue of birth and/or by allegiance to the monarchy proven on fields of battle.

Mercantilism

Mercantilism is the second economic system of note, because it takes the basic tenets of feudalism and couples them with the developments made possible by the Age of Exploration in Europe. This would include the subjugation of many foreign lands, and the displacement of indigenous systems of commerce, with colonialism. Under mercantilism and colonialism, the prominence of the isolation of the manor that was attendant with feudalism gives way to the growth of the city-state. It is with the growth of the city-state that there also begins the growth of the nation-state. "For God and country," became the cry, and the method of extraction gained from the complexity of things like Triangular Trade.

In Triangular Trade, there are the three components of mother country, an Old World colony, and a New World colony. From the mother country, ships are built to be the vessels of trade under mercantilism. Thus, for instance, a ship is built in the English port town of Liverpool. That cargo ship is filled with weapons of destruction, such as small firearms. It is with these trading implements that natives will be encouraged to subdue each other. The ship sails to Africa, where the guns are traded for slaves. Now, the cargo has been switched, so that a human cargo will be transported to the Caribbean, where they will be off-loaded. Then, the empty vessel is reloaded with goods such as tobacco, sugar, rum, cotton, and/or rice, which are available only in the New World. Those goods are then shipped back for the enrichment of the mother country. It is this sort of trade that was at the heart of the writings of John Locke. In Locke's own famous words, "government should rest upon the dominion of property."

The economic system of mercantilism resulted in the worldwide under-development of the colonies, and the prosperity of many European nations. The continuing deleterious impact on so-called "Third World" countries is quite evident, but also quite denied. For example, estimations of the number of African lives lost during the TranAtlantic Slave Trade range from twenty to 100 million.

Capitalism

Finally, the economic system that will be reviewed later in this text is capitalism. But, it is of extreme importance that students of American government understand how capitalism developed as an economic system. Frequently students articulate an orientation about economics as if capitalism either always existed, or as if it sprang forth as a fully developed entity. Nothing could be farther than the reality of the interconnectedness of these economic systems. As a reminder, students should be acutely aware that the philosophical text upon which capitalism was founded was not published until 1776. In other words, Adam Smith's *An Inquiry into the Nature and Causes of the Wealth of Nations* was written at the dawn of the Industrial Revolution, not at the dawn of time itself.

Jamestown Settlement

Therefore, keeping an accurate historical timeline is essential to a fuller understanding of the social milieu of Colonial America. Recent studies of an array of evidences have revealed that the first experiences of the British outcasts in the New World were not as laudable as many of us have been taught. But, beyond the myths there are discernible facts. Whether one chooses to rely on the traditional story of 20 Africans among the many indentured servants, or of the 32 Africans who were listed in the Virginia Census of 1619 five months earlier, it is clear that an African presence was a part of the Jamestown Settlement. More notable is the fact that, within 50 years, Virginia had deteriorated into a slaveholding colony. And, as the first British colony, Virginia set the standard for slavery as a race-based institution, backed by the power and force of the British crown. Besides this, at no point in American history did more than 25% of whites own slaves. Moreover, nearly nine of ten slaveholders had fewer than twenty slaves. This is remarkable in order to dispel two enduring myths about American slavery: the first is that slave ownership was widespread among whites; and the second is that the archetypical slaveholding enterprise was a large plantation. This data makes perfect sense, because owning a human being was a costly venture that most could not afford. This is true, not only in terms of purchase, but also in terms of care and maintenance. Accordingly, owning many slaves could be possible only for the very wealthy.

If it seems as if matters have strayed off topic, I want the reader to recall that the economic systems, whether they be feudalism, mercantilism/colonialism, or capitalism, tend to benefit those who possess economic strength. And, those with economic strength tend to advocate for the enhancement of their own interests, just as is true of any other group or class. When one amalgamates this information, it begins to make more sense that the wealthy elites who founded the United States of America were the direct descendants of the wealthy elites who established colonies for the British crown. Most of the "rank and file" may have been those who were cast aside due to their religious convictions, but the leaders of the colonies were well-heeled elites. With the exception of the Society of Friends (Quakers) in Pennsylvania, most of those religious convictions did not even include the equal treatment of all human beings.

Plymouth Settlement

Nonetheless, the significance of the Jamestown, Virginia, settlement rests on its being the first established by the British in North America. But, it is the Plymouth, Massachusetts, settlement that truly set the stage for the eventual founding of the American body politic. This claim is buttressed by the Mayflower Compact, which was signed on 11 November 1620. The compact is strong evidence of the nascent application of the concept of "consent of the governed," decades before any influence from Hobbes, Locke, or Rousseau. However, history has conveniently failed to remind us that, out of over 100 possible signatories, only 41 men actually signed the Mayflower Compact. This undoubtedly undermines any validity to the notion that the Massachusetts Bay Colony was a democratic venture. That is not surprising, taking into consideration that the leaders of the colony were anti democratic.

Puritanism

One of the most enduring concepts in this country is something known as "American exceptionalism." The religious and moral underpinnings of the United States can be traced back through the Pilgrims to the Puritans. The Puritans were the most dominant religious group in Colonial America. Although there are several basic principles that Puritans followed, it is most important to know that they believed in the rule of God over all things. As a matter of personality, John Calvin, and what has been deemed *Calvinism,* are very instructive. Calvinism taught the sinfulness of man, the even greater sinfulness of women, a strong belief in hard work and meritocracy, and predestination. Predestination claimed that God was the only determiner of the fate of humans, and of who would be saved from the original sin into which all humans were born. It is not difficult to extrapolate how enslaving Africans, or wiping out natives, could be justified under that interpretation of Christianity.

Through that window shines the terminology of a former Governor of the Massachusetts Bay Colony by the name of John Winthrop. This religious and political leader declared that the Puritans were part of a pact with God to create a holy community in the New World. He characterized this community as a "city on a hill," which was to become a beacon to the entire world. But for Winthrop, this shining light was not to be democratic. In his own words: "A democracy is, amongst civil nations, accounted the meanest and worst of all forms of government." It is ironic that the person credited with articulating the claim of American exceptionalism was fervently anti democratic.

American Exceptionalism

The person credited with coining the term "American exceptionalism" was the Frenchman Alexis de Tocqueville. The title of his 1835 seminal text was *Democracy in America.* Briefly stated, this concept rests on the contention that America occupies a unique place among nations on this earth. It is comparable to the concept of Manifest Destiny in the 1840s. In both cases, the expansion of the country was thought to be an extension of the will of God. Today, we find the same mentality among many Americans. Frequently it is articulated as America being the best country in the world. Or, it can take the form that America is the purveyor of democracy for the entire world. There are any number of variations on the theme. Later in this text, we will address the connections between "American exceptionalism," ideology, and neoconservatism.

Colonial Economies

Colonial America was not a monolithic entity. Most historians separate the 13 colonies into 3 specific geographic areas. There were the New England colonies, such as New Hampshire, Massachusetts, Rhode Island, and Connecticut. There were the Middle Colonies, such as New York, New Jersey, Pennsylvania, and Delaware. And there were the Southern Colonies, such as Maryland, Virginia, the Carolinas, and Georgia. Each region had its own economic propensities. For example, the New England colonies were based on fishing and farming along the rivers, timber inland, due to the rocky soil, and shipbuilding along the coast. The Middle Colonies were based on grains grown in rich soil, textiles milled by the diversity of European immigrants to the colony, and timber and ship-building, due to the availability of deep-water ports such as those of New York City and Philadelphia. Because of the diversity of the Middle Colonies, they were the most socially tolerant. The Southern Colonies were dominated by the cash crops of tobacco, cotton, rice, indigo, and sugar cane. Because these crops were extremely labor intensive, the Southern Colonies were dependent on mostly slave labor.

Slavery

Although slavery proved most intractable in the Southern Colonies, it existed throughout all of the colonies. What first became institutionalized by the Virginia Legislature in 1662, would not end until over 200 years later. To their credit, several states abolished slavery during the 1780s. The states that abolished slavery were Pennsylvania in 1780, Connecticut and Rhode Island in 1784, New York in 1785, and New Jersey in 1786. It is no coincidence, however, that the states that first abolished slavery were not economically dependent on the peculiar institution.

Perhaps the most troubling omission from many American government texts is the failure to grant any significant treatment to the opposition to slavery that existed during colonial times. Many students of American government are duped into thinking that slavery was more widely accepted than it actually was. Long lost in the annals of American history is the anti slavery rhetoric of Jefferson's first draft of the Declaration of Independence. Also lost is the long history of rebellions and insurrections against slavery that included slave and non slave participants. In addition, there has been a lack of recognition of the presence of thousands of Africans who were either never slaves, or who had been manumitted. Shameful is the absence in most American government texts of the first to fall in the cause of American freedom. Crispus Attucks was the first man shot in the Boston Massacre, on 5 March 1770. He was a forty-seven-year-old runaway slave from Framingham, Massachusetts. Even more disturbing is the usual absence of mention of the "free" Blacks who served on both sides of the Revolutionary War. Two, by the names of Prince Whipple and Oliver Cromwell, were in the boat with General George Washington as he (now famously) crossed the Delaware River. Another, by the name of Prince Hall, founded the Black Masons in 1794 in Boston. Two others, by the names of Richard Allen (who purchased his and his brother's freedom at age 17) and Absalom Jones, founded the African Methodist Episcopal Church in 1787 in Philadelphia. The land Richard Allen purchased to build the first Black church in America is still the longest continuously Black-owned plot of real estate in our history. These Black Methodists played key roles in fighting slavery. In fact, after the 1822 insurrection in Charleston, South Carolina, was led by a Black Methodist preacher by the name of Denmark Vesey, the Black Church was crushed in the antebellum Southern Colonies.

In other words, in Colonial America, events that contributed to the founding of the republic have been largely whitewashed. In 1656 in Massachusetts, and in 1660 in Connecticut, the fear of slave insurrections caused the passage of laws excluding Blacks from joining militias. The first record of a slave uprising is of one in New York in 1712, followed by a larger multiracial insurrection in 1741. In 1739, there was the Stono Rebellion near Charleston, South Carolina. In 1742, seven Black cooks were executed for poisoning their masters in Maryland. There are many more undeniable examples of significant events in Colonial America, and it is difficult to gain a fuller understanding of the issues at play during the Constitutional Conventions without this pertinent information.

Continental Conflict

The French and Indian War (1754–1763) was the first significant exposure of the discord between the British Crown and the American Colonies. The contention arose not so much because of the war itself, but because of the royal attempts to tax the colonists to pay for it. This controversy began in 1764, with the passage of various Acts. As a partial listing, there was the 1764 Sugar Act, the 1765 Stamp Act, the 1765 Quartering Act, the 1767 Townshend Acts, the 1773 Tea Act, and the 1774 so-called Intolerable Acts. The imposition of taxes by the British Parliament through these Acts raised the call against "taxation without representation." In 1768, the British military sought to quell dissent by occupying Boston. Attempting to control this hotbed of protest proved too difficult. What followed was the Boston Massacre, which in turn led to the Boston Tea Party, in December of 1773. This brazen display of insolent disregard for the authority of the British Crown resulted in passage of the Intolerable Acts. Boston Harbor was closed, and the colony was placed under direct British rule. At that point, revolution was just around the corner.

The colonists' response to the Intolerable Acts was to convene two Continental Congresses, between September 1774 and May 1775. By the time of the Second Congress, open military hostilities had broken out near Boston. Throughout the Revolutionary War, the Second Continental Congress met and fashioned a government. In 1777, the Articles of Confederation were offered to the thirteen colonies for ratification. It took until 1781. By 1783, the Treaty of Paris was signed, and the war was over. For the new country there was much work to be done.

Nascent Years of the New Republic

The Articles of Confederation lasted less than ten years. The governing body was called the Congress of the Confederation, and it had one ambassador from each state. What it did have was dwarfed by what it did not have, though. For instance, it did not have effective powers of relating with foreign states. It could not regulate interstate commerce, nor could it raise a standing army. It did manage to unanimously pass the Northwest Ordinance of 1787, which established the specter of new states without slavery. The Northwest Ordinance also provided for some of the same civil rights later adopted in the Bill of Rights. However, the inadequacies and weaknesses of the Articles of Confederation were revealed by an event in American history that must be given its due because of its extraordinary impact on the need to solidify the power of the American government.

Shays Rebellion

In the late summer of 1786, unruly mobs began to riot around Springfield, Massachusetts. Within months, Shays's Rebellion would instill fear into the hearts of the propertied class of the new republic. Lead by former Captain Daniel Shays of the former Revolutionary Army, the basis of this uprising was the treatment of debtors by the court system. The confiscation of property and the imprisonment of these poor farmers proved too much to bear for the young nation. Many of the debtors had risked their lives in the fight against tyranny. Now they were being forced to carry the heavy burden of the postwar economy. They faced high land taxes, a slumping economy, and exorbitant legal fees to defend their property rights. These factors pushed their frustration level beyond reason. In response, the rebels sought to disrupt the court proceedings that would otherwise result in the loss of their lands. Their attacks on the court system were largely nonviolent. In most cases, several hundred to several thousand men would show up on court dates and disrupt the proceedings. The militia that formed to snuff out the rebellion was bankrolled by moneyed interests, and it evinced a class warfare that struck terror into the protectors of the status quo. The depiction of crazed debtors appears today to be hyperbole. This is because there were no reported casualties until the end of Shays's Rebellion, even though it lasted five months (1786–1787).

Whichever rendering one seeks to adopt, there is little question that Shays's Rebellion provided the impetus to alter the structure and function of the American government. Within months, there appeared the Constitutional Convention in Philadelphia, and the publication of the Federalist Papers in New York City. The quest for liberty that had begun nearly two centuries before was about to create the longest-standing democratic republic in human history.

Chapter 2
Study Guide

1. Historically, the major division in American politics has been over
   _____ issues.
   - a: political
   - (b:) racial
   - c: economic
   - d: health care

2. A league of <u>independent</u> states, where the central government has only those matters expressly delegated to it is a:
   - a: democratic system
   - b: federal system
   - (c:) unitary system
   - d: confederate system

3. Which slaveholding "founding father" is the author of the Declaration of Independence?
   - a: Washington
   - b: Roosevelt
   - c: Hamilton
   - (d:) Jefferson
   - e: Adams

4. To the framers of the Constitution, the appeal of <u>federalism</u> was that it:
   - a: allowed the states to control the process of government decision-making
   - (b:) retained state traditions and local power while it established a strong national government
   - c: was acceptable to the British Parliament
   - d: did not change the status quo

5. Shay's Rebellion demonstrated that the central government:
   - a: had the capability to protect citizens from riots and civil unrest
   - b: dared not confront the state militias
   - c: could easily incite citizens to riot
   - (d:) did not care about the welfare of the people
   - e: could not protect the citizenry from armed rebellion

6. The Declaration of Independence is:

a: beautifully written

b: a sham

c: an amendable document

(d:) a long list of grievances

7. "American Exceptionalism" as coined by Alexis de Tocqueville manifests today in the articulation that:

a: America is the worst country in the world

(b:) America is the best country in the world

c: America is no different than any other country

d: America has seen its best days

CHAPTER 3

Constructing Columbia's Covenant

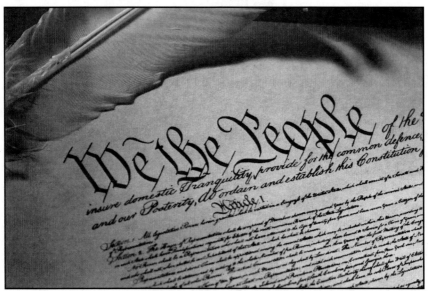

Image © James Steidl, 2009. Used under license from Shutterstock, Inc.

Federalist Paper 51

It took a considerable amount of lobbying to convince the American body politic that what is now known as the U.S. Constitution should be adopted. To this end, there were eighty-five articles written by three authors. Future Secretary of the Treasury Alexander Hamilton wrote fifty-one; future President James Madison wrote twenty-nine; and future Supreme Court Chief Justice John Jay wrote five. But of all the Federalist Papers, the one that stood out most in terms of the structure of the American government was "FP 51." This Madisonian model of government is so fundamental to an evaluation of our republic that basic political science courses should use the model as a measurement of the operation of our government today. The adherence to the Madisonian model has been stronger and weaker at different times in American history. James Madison laid out a framework that promoted a system of structural checks and balances for our government. This also included the concept of the separation of powers. For this James Madison is known as the "Father of the Constitution."

Checks and Balances

The structure of the U.S. government is that of a republic, not that of a democracy. In a democracy, the people rule. In a republican form of government, the people elect those who rule. Madison considered a republic to require different branches of government, with the legislature strongest. However, a strong legislature that was only popularly elected was a scary prospect for members of the elite class, such as the founders. Hence, the national legislature was broken into two components. The term for this in political science parlance is bicameralism. The U.S. Congress was broken into two distinct chambers, with distinct powers, terms, and eligibility requirements. The check and the balance are evidenced in several ways. For one, the members of what can be aptly described as the lower chamber (the House of Representatives) are popularly elected by the people according to proportional representation. Conversely, the members of what can be aptly described as the upper chamber (the Senate) were initially selected by each state's legislature. This was to "check," or balance popular will against elite power. It should be noted that it took the passage of the 17th Amendment in 1913 to submit the election of Senators to a popular vote.

Another check and balance is not within one branch of government, but involves the interaction between the branches of government. Structurally, the American government has 3 branches. They are the Legislature, the Executive, and the Judiciary. These 3 branches are able to check and balance each other through the constitutional powers given to them. For example, the legislative branch can check the executive branch through its power to allocate funds, override vetoes, and initiate investigations. The executive branch can check the legislative branch through policy implementation, and tools such as the veto. The judicial branch can check either the legislative or the executive branch through its interpretation (judicial review) of laws, and the Constitution. The legislative branch can check the judicial branch through impeachment, the control of its structure, the Senate's responsibility to give advice and consent with relation to executive appointments, and the constitutional amendment process. The executive branch can check the judicial branch through the control of appointments. The combinations of the exertion of checks and balances within one branch, or between two branches of government, are quite numerous.

Separation of Powers

The Madisonian model also called for the separation of powers of the 3 branches of government. Simply put, the Legislature was given the power to create laws. The Executive was given the power to enforce laws. The Judiciary was given the power to interpret laws. The entire body politic was considered to be operating under the very basic notion that we are a nation of laws, not of men. As such, this is a civil society, where no one is above the law. Madison's vision is plainly seen in the structure of the U.S. Constitution. It has 7 articles, and the first 3 cover the areas of the people, as represented by the Article I focus on the Congress; the leader, as represented by the Article II focus on the Presidency; and the interpreter, as represented by the Article III focus on the Judiciary.

The separation of powers is embodied in each of the first three Articles describing the inherent powers of the particular branch. In Article I, there are over a dozen enumerated powers of Congress. There is even a "catch-all" that is sometimes referred to as the "elastic clause," which states that Congress has the power to go beyond what has been enumerated if it is "necessary and proper" to do so. In Article II, there are several responsibilities placed upon the Executive that are not associated with the Congress. In Article III, there is more vagueness, but over time the role of the courts has become solidified. In understanding the structure of the American government, it is essential to know that, although each branch has a specific sphere of influence, there is overlap of the powers in some areas. This overlap has been the subject of great interest and debate among constitutional scholars and laypersons alike. Therefore, it is more sensible to think about the separation of powers as interlocking mechanisms of one machine, rather than as independent mechanisms of three machines.

Congress

The structure of Congress is dominated by rule by committee. This is true whether one is examining the House or the Senate. The House has 435 members, who are distributed among the fifty states. The House is configured according to the principle of proportional representation. Every ten years since 1790, the American government conducts a U.S. Census, which determines (among other things) the number of inhabitants of an area, and shifts in population. Hence, while the House will continue to have 435 seats, how those seats will be allocated to and within each state is based on the demographic findings of the Census. However, each state is guaranteed through Article I of the U.S. Constitution at least one seat in the House, regardless of how small its population may be. The most populous state (California) has fifty-three seats, which is (correspondingly) the largest delegation.

Article I of the Constitution set three basic eligibility requirements for a citizen to become a member of the House. The citizen must be at least twenty-five years of age, have lived in the U.S. at least seven years, and be a resident of the state she or he seeks to represent in the Congress. The term of service is two years. This means that every even-numbered calendar year, all 435 members of the House are up for election or reelection. Several years ago, individual states attempted to set term limits on how long a person could serve in the Congress, but those efforts were repudiated by the U.S. Supreme Court as unconstitutional.

The Senate has the constant number (as long as there are fifty states) of 100. Each state (irrespective of geographical size or population) has two senators. Again, Article I set three basic eligibility requirements for a citizen to become a member of the Senate. The citizen must be at least thirty years of age, have lived in the U.S. for at least nine years, and be a resident of the state she or he seeks to represent in the Congress. U.S. senators serve six-year terms. This means that every even numbered calendar year one-third of the Senate is up for election or reelection. Like the House, members of the Senate can serve as long as they are chosen to serve by the people of their respective states. There have been members of Congress who have served for several decades.

There are four types of committees in the Congress. There are standing committees, select committees, joint committees, and conference committees. Conference committees are really joint committees, but they are "ad hoc" in the sense that they exist only to refine (eliminate the differences in the House and Senate versions of) a specific piece of potential legislation that has been passed in both chambers. Currently there are twenty standing committees in the House, with one Permanent Select Committee, and 104 subcommittees. In the Senate there are sixteen standing committees, four non standing committees, with 73 subcommittees.

Because of the Senate tradition of unlimited debate, the procedural tool known as the filibuster must be addressed. A filibuster occurs when a senator uses the debate forum as a means to prevent a vote on a bill. All that is required is for the senator to talk while remaining in the same spot. The record for a filibuster in the U.S. Senate was set by Strom Thurmond (D/R, SC) in his failed effort to prevent passage of the Civil Rights Act of 1957. That act sought voting rights for Blacks, to which Senator Thurmond was vehemently opposed. He talked continuously for 24 hours, 18 minutes, and he spoke of his grandmother's biscuit recipe and read from the phone book. Although it rarely prevents such absurdities, the Senate passed Rule twenty-two in 1917. This rule allowed cloture (the closing of debate) if two-thirds of senators present voted in favor. In 1975, Rule twenty-two reduced the number of senators needed to vote in favor of cloture to three-fifths of senators present.

Because of our two-party-dominated winner-take-all system, the major party that controls the chamber also controls all of the committees in that chamber. This means that because 234 of the 435 members of the House are Republicans, that party gets to control the Speaker of the House position and all committees through membership and chairpersonship. Accordingly, because fifty-two of the 100 members of the Senate are Democrats, that party gets to control the Senate Majority Leader position and all the committees through membership and chairpersonship. Additionally, the two Senators who are "Independents" (Angus King of Maine, and Bernie Sanders of Vermont) caucus with the Democrats. For the most part, rising to chair a committee or take a congressional leadership role is based on seniority.

However, even members without seniority can be placed on powerful and desirable committees if the leadership of that chamber deems such an appointment advantageous for their party, or for their party's agenda. It should be noted that if one of the two major parties garners enough of a majority in a chamber of Congress, it is tantamount to one-party rule. In the case of the House, that would mean reaching a two-thirds majority of at least 291 members. In the case of the Senate, that would mean reaching a two-thirds majority of at least sixty-seven members, or a filibuster-proof three-fifths majority of at least sixty members. The implications of either the fact of a majority, or of the size of a majority, are enormous. In terms of the fact of a majority, there are stronger implications when there is no divided government. Divided government occurs when the party that controls either or both chambers of the Congress is different from the party of the Executive. When there is divided government, the likelihood of cooperation on a legislative agenda is rather low. When there is no divided government, vetoes are more rare, and the significance of the legislation that passes tends to be higher. On another note, there has been improvement in the diversity of the Senate. In this 113th Congress, there are 20 women Senators, and a paltry, but improved two Black members. The number of women serving in the United States Senate is the largest in American history. As a matter of design, the Congress is supposed to come to a compromised resolution of the issues of the day. The paradox of our current circumstance is debilitating because if one political party is able to "muscle" a bill through, the eventual undermining of the legislative effort will be achieved. As an example, although the Patient Protection and Affordable Care Act was ruled constitutional by the Supreme Court in June, 2012, the social, political, and legal challenges have rendered the Act virtually unworkable. The pejoratively called "Obamacare" was pushed through Congress with precious little bipartisan support.

The national election results from November, 2012 make it more likely that the 113th Congress may very well be more of a "do nothing" Congress than the dismal legislative record of the 112th.

The Executive

When most Americans think of the executive branch, they think of the President of the United States. Although this is understandable, the executive branch also encompasses the federal bureaucracy. But, what are the qualifications for our highest office? Article II of the U.S. Constitution outlines just three requirements to be eligible to be the Commander in Chief. One must be a natural born citizen, be at least thirty-five years of age, and have resided in the United States for (at least) the previous fourteen years. Also, a person can be elected only to two four-year terms. It is possible to serve longer, if a person succeeds into office and serves out less than half of her or his predecessor's term. The same three requirements hold true for the Vice President, whose only constitutional role is as the President of the Senate. That responsibility is frequently delegated to a leadership position known as Senate President Pro Tempore. Normally, the Senate President Pro Tempore is the longest serving member of the party in the majority in the Senate. Beyond the largely ceremonial title for the Vice President, the person who is Vice President does have the power to vote in the Senate, but only in the event of a 50–50 tie. That situation does occasionally present itself.

The size and scope of presidential power is difficult to glean from reviewing the sparse wording in Article II. It takes a look at American history to begin to fully comprehend the inherent powers of the Executive. To begin, the responsibilities of the office must be understood. The President of the

United States is at once the Commander in Chief of the Armed Forces; the diplomatic Head of State; the leader of her or his political party; plainly put, the President is the leader of this nation.

As the country has grown and developed, so has the Executive Branch. However, it is essential to grasp that the expansion of the power of the presidency has been an undulation. As all Americans know, there are some presidents who are more notable than others. In some cases this is due to the actions of the individual "Chief," and in others it is due to circumstances far beyond one powerful man's ambit of influence. The details of the most significant contributors to the lore of the Oval Office will be provided in Chapter 5 of this manual.

Structurally, the Executive Branch is composed of three distinct entities. First, there is the Executive Office of the President. Second, there are the Cabinet Departments. Third, there are Agencies and Government Corporations. Together, these are known as the Federal Bureaucracy. Without getting into a Weberian analysis, it is most important to understand that these bureaucracies control policy development and implementation. Most of the development of policy emanates from the Oval but as witnessed during both administrations under George W. Bush, significant policy can be developed from the Office of the Vice President. But, the amount of power wielded by Dick Cheney as Vice President will probably not be seen again for some time. After a full administrative term, current Vice President Joe Biden shows no designs on being the policy-maker that Dick Cheney was.

The President's Cabinet

There are fifteen Departments that the Executive oversees. Some of them harken back to the very beginning of the Republic. For instance, what is now called the Department of State was formerly known as the Department of Foreign Affairs. All of these cabinet positions except the Justice Department are headed by what are known as "Secretaries." The head of the Justice Department is the Attorney General of the United States. The head of the Department of State is known as the Secretary of State, and is fourth in line of succession to the presidency. This is because the Constitution calls (after the Vice President, Speaker of the House, and Senate President Pro Tempore) for the line of succession to follow the Departments in the order that they became Cabinet level positions in the Executive Branch. According to that formulaic, the Secretary of the Department of Homeland Security would be last in line of succession as far as Cabinet level posts are concerned, because that department is the newest.

Alphabetically, the Cabinet Departments are: Agriculture, Commerce, Defense, Education, Energy, Health and Human Services, Homeland Security, Housing and Urban Development, Interior, Justice, Labor, State, Transportation, Treasury, and Veteran Affairs. Each head of a cabinet department is appointed by the President of the United States, and must be confirmed by the United States Senate. Each also serves at the behest and pleasure of the President, and can be removed without process.

Agencies

There are too many agencies to mention, but highlighting some that should be familiar to most Americans is useful. Again, these are the compartmentalized entities that make and implement federal policy. As related to foreign affairs, Americans will have heard of the Central Intelligence Agency (CIA). As related to clean air or water, Americans will have heard of the Environmental Protection Agency (EPA). As related to the media, Americans will have heard of the Federal Communications Commission (FCC). As related to natural disasters (especially after Hurricane Katrina), Americans will have heard of the Federal Emergency Management Agency (FEMA). As related to the money and credit supply, Americans will have heard of the Federal Reserve System. As related to space travel, Americans will have heard of the National Aeronautics and Space Administration (NASA). As related to public television, some Americans will have heard of the Corporation for Public Broadcasting, the National Endowment for the Arts, or the National Endowment for the Humanities. As related to train travel, Americans probably are unfamiliar with the National Railroad Passenger Corporation, but they have heard of its acronym AMTRAK.

Add to the above the Peace Corps, the SEC, the SBA, the SSA, and the USPS, and you should have some idea of how vast the federal bureaucracy is. But, not all agencies enjoy the same status. Some are independent agencies that exist without Cabinet level clout. NASA, or the SBA, would fall into that category. Other agencies are regulatory agencies that also lack Cabinet level clout, but for a different reason. Because their focus is on the implementation of policy, regulatory agencies are created by Congress, and they are staffed largely by nonpartisans.

Despite the Clinton Administration's (largely through Vice President Al Gore) near heroic efforts to promote bureaucratic accountability through "Reinventing Government," if both civilian and military are tallied up, the

Federal Bureaucracy employs over 5 million people. It should be understood that with that many people working in all the agencies involved, there is bound to be waste and inefficiency. During the Reagan years over a quarter a century ago, there were serious attempts to downsize the federal bureaucracy. Whether the approach used is privatization, deregulation, or something else, the Executive Branch continues to grapple with this behemoth. This dying monster was given new life after the attacks on the United States on 11 September 2001. Not only was a Cabinet level position added, the Department of Homeland Security shifted FEMA from an independent agency to one under control of the Executive, moved the Secret Service and the U.S. Customs Service from the Department of the Treasury, moved the Immigration and Naturalization Service from the Department of Justice, and placed the U.S. Coast Guard under its aegis. Inevitably, many billions of dollars flowed to this new Cabinet Department that was charged with protecting the nation, and the bureaucracy was fattening once again.

Inherent Powers

Exactly what powers a president has is a thorny topic. Attempts to characterize them as "inherent" should be understood as a matter of constitutional interpretation. There is no doubt that various presidents have made disparate claims of inherent power. As a matter of interpretation, students are encouraged to read the Constitution as one document. This is due to the fact that there are those who would seek to accord more or less power to the Executive based upon their own political agenda. If one reads the entire Constitution in concert, it is clear that Article I lays out many enumerated powers for Congress. However, in Article II we are left to interpret one vague sentence in section 1: "The executive power shall be vested in a President of the United States of America." From that simple declarative statement some have argued the preposterous. This would include something known as the "unitary executive theory," which has been used to subvert the checks and balances of the Madisonian Model. An example would be the G. W. Bush Administration's claim of the ability to ignore long-standing traditions such as the availability of the extraordinary writ of habeas corpus, and respecting the Geneva Conventions as related to the treatment of prisoners of war. To claim that a wartime president has the power to sweep aside judicial and congressional oversight based on the first sentence of Article II, section 1, has been a disturbing nightmare for many Americans. It is not enough to change labels, and the Supreme Court has met its charge as the final arbiter of constitutionality. The damage to the prestige of the office (not the individual person) of the President of the United States is still being assessed. Thinly veiled is the reality that calling a prisoner of war an "enemy combatant" does not change the limits on sub-human treatment. Even more thinly veiled is changing the label from tor-ture to "enhanced interrogation techniques." Attempting to reclassify unacceptable practices by renaming them to sound like a really fun and exciting extreme sport (e.g., "waterboarding") has left more than a few constitutional scholars aghast.

Beyond that which is controversial, Article II, section 3, requires the President to report to Congress "from time to time." Traditionally, that has become known as the "State of the Union" address, which is given at the beginning of every calendar year. Article II, section 4, directs the basis of removal of a sitting President. Treason and bribery are some-what easy to interpret, but what qualifies as "other high crimes and mis-demeanors" has proven to be more difficult. Only twice in our nation's history has impeachment of a President occurred. On both occasions the Senate failed to provide the necessary two-thirds vote for conviction. In 1868, Andrew Johnson escaped conviction by one vote. Thirty-five senators voted to convict, and 19 voted not guilty of high crimes and misdemeanors. In 1999, Bill Clinton escaped conviction, and the vote was not nearly as close. The Senate voted 55 not guilty, 45 guilty on the charge of perjury, and 50 not guilty, 50 guilty on the charge of obstruc-tion of justice. As a reminder, it would have taken 67 senators to vote guilty in order for Bill Clinton to have been successfully impeached.

Ironically, at the heart of the Johnson impeachment was an issue related to inherent powers. Whether the claim that Johnson's violation of the Tenure of Office Act was legitimately "other high crimes and misde-meanors" is dubious at best. In fact, not only was the Act repealed by Congress in 1887, a later Supreme Court case made it clear that the President has the power to remove political appointees. As was true in the Clinton impeachment, the motives to impeach were largely political. Yet, no matter what the motives, the issue of the inherent powers of the President will continue to call into question the viability of an "imperial presidency."

The Judiciary

The judicial branch of the federal government is under the rather loose parameters described in the U.S. Constitution, Article III. Unbeknown to many Americans, the Constitution specifies only that there be one supreme court, and leaves it to Congress to determine any lesser courts. With the exception of the vagueness of Article II, section 1, as related to the power of the executive, Article III arguably leaves the most room for interpretation or misinterpretation of the founders' intent. Not only is there a lack of specifics for the composition of the judicial branch, there is not even a number of members proscribed for the one supreme court. Hence, during the history of the nation, the membership of the Supreme Court has fluctuated mostly between five and nine. Under the second Franklin Roosevelt administration, the president unsuccessfully attempted to expand the size of the Court's membership to as large as fifteen. The size of the modern Court has settled on nine members since 1869, but it should be understood that this is more a matter of tradition than constitutional requirement.

Accordingly, although Article III, section 2, did outline some bases for the judiciary to have jurisdiction in a case, vagueness continued to prevail. Jurisdiction is the power necessary for a court to hear any case. It is broken into two components: subject matter jurisdiction, and personal jurisdiction. Both must be present for a court to have the power to hear and rule on a case. Ironically, the altogether inescapable issue of jurisdiction was one of those things that is not clearly enunciated in the U.S. Constitution. It took an assertive court under the leadership of Chief Justice John Marshall to carve out the Supreme Court's power to be the final arbiter of legal disputes. The Marshall Court did so in the landmark 1803 case of *Marbury v. Madison,* where it established the power of judicial review.

The structure of the judiciary did not truly take shape until the passage of the Judiciary Act of 1789. This Act of Congress established a Supreme Court with 5 justices and 1 Chief Justice, circuits that justices had to "ride," and district courts that were, and continue to be, trial-level courts in the federal system. Circuit riding took place for over 100 years, and it made becoming a Supreme Court justice less than appealing to many in the legal profession. One has only to imagine the exhaustions of travel in the late 18th and 19th centuries to understand the rigors involved. For the first 102 years of the federal court system, circuits were also trial-level courts. Today, there are thirteen Circuit Courts of Appeal in the federal system. Twelve of them are based on geographic region, and the other is called the Federal Circuit. There are eleven Circuit Courts that are enumerated, and the twelfth is called the D.C. Circuit. This last mentioned circuit is not to be confused with the Federal Circuit, even though the Federal Circuit is located in Washington, D.C. The Federal Circuit was not created until 1982. It hears appeals from what are called specialized courts. Some examples of specialized courts include subjects such as Veteran Affairs, Copyrights and Trademarks, and International Trade. The Federal Circuit is the only circuit that bases its jurisdiction on subject matter, and not merely geography.

The Ninth Circuit, which is headquartered in San Francisco, California, is by far the largest circuit. It covers more geography, and it has jurisdiction over at least twice as large a population as any other circuit. In fact, it has over 20% of the U.S. population under its charge. However, the most influential circuit is the D.C. Circuit. A judge sitting on the D.C. Circuit is more likely to have to confront legal issues that have the broadest, and deepest political ramifications. This is because it is the appellate court for events that occur in the nation's capital. Altogether, there are nearly 200 judgeships in the U.S. Courts of Appeals. The circuit courts have been the most frequent stepping stones for appointment to the U.S. Supreme Court.

As mentioned, the trial courts in the federal judiciary are called district courts. These courts are administered according to judicial districts. There are ninety-four such districts distributed throughout the fifty states. They deploy nearly 700 federal judges. No matter what level of the federal judiciary, all judges or justices serve life terms. They must be appointed by the President of the United States, and confirmed by a simple majority of the U.S. Senate. And, in order to remove any one of them, the judge must be successfully impeached, just like the President must be. This does not happen often, but it does happen. Allegations of violation of the constitutional requirement of good behavior, is usually at the center of the impeachment proceedings against a federal judge.

Many Americans are familiar with the colloquial expression "don't make a federal case of it." How did that phrase enter and remain in the American vernacular? It is because there are far fewer federal crimes than state crimes, and the most easily understood basis for initiating a federal case is if there is a federal question involved. But, that is not the only means to have your case heard in federal court. Original jurisdiction can come through a case where citizens of two or more different states are parties to a lawsuit. If the matter involves more than $75,000, then diversity jurisdiction exists, and the case can be heard in federal court. Also, if the United States is a party to the case, it can be heard in federal court.

Finally, many Americans wonder how a case makes its way all the way to the U.S. Supreme Court. It is not necessary for a case to start in the federal court system to end up in our highest court. For the most part, the Supreme

Court is a court of what is called appellate jurisdiction. That means that the case has been heard by a lower court, and one of the parties appeals that lower court's decision to the Supreme Court. More than at any time in American history, the Supreme Court determines which cases it will hear. The Judiciary Act of 1925 enabled the Court to exert control over its docket. This is done through what is known as the "rule of four." Most of the cases that the Court hears come by virtue of a writ of certiorari. This Latin term roughly translates into "to be shown." Because there is no right of appeal to the U.S. Supreme Court, it takes four of the nine justices to agree to hear a case. In any given calendar year, the Court, by granting the writ of certiorari, hears approximately 1% of those cases requesting for review. The Court tends to take cases where there is a conflict of judicial interpretation between circuits, or where an issue is of great contemporary importance. Additionally, the Supreme Court, by virtue of Article III and the Judiciary Act of 1789, is able to have original jurisdiction where ambassadors or other foreign representatives are involved, or when one state sues another, or when a state sues the United States.

Perhaps the most important thing to understand about the Supreme Court is its limitation in terms of power. When compared to the other two branches of the federal government, the Supreme Court is most reliant on the Madisonian Model for its effectiveness. After all, the Court is rarely successful at legislating from the bench, and it has no enforcement powers. Nonetheless, it is the single most important institution, along with the other aspects of the federal judiciary, that protects America's ability to claim to be a civil society under the rule of law, with equal justice for all.

Chapter 3
Study Guide

1. What is the main subject discussed in Madison's Federalist Paper No. 51?

   a: separation of powers

   b: factions

   c: the Declaration of Independence

   d: political parties

   e: the Madisonian Model

2. What is the main subject discussed in Madison's Federalist Paper #10?

   a: friction

   b: interdiction

   c: factions

   d: actions

   e: political parties

3. The Great Compromise:

   a: resulted in the Bill of Rights being added to the Constitution

   b: broke the deadlock between the large and small states over the nature of representation in the new national government

   c: established the Electoral College as the vehicle for electing the president

   d: allowed George Washington to be nominated and elected the first president

4. Name the 3 authors of the Federalist Papers:

   a: Tinkers, Evers, Chance

   b: Washington, Adams, Paine

   c: Burr, Hamilton, Adams

   d: Hamilton, Jay, Madison

   e: Roosevelt, Lincoln, Jefferson

5. Identify the number of Articles and Amendments (respectively) to the U.S. Constitution:

   a: 7/17

   b: 10/20

   c: 3/25

   d: 10/23

   e: 7/27

6. The Madisonian Model of a government scheme refers to:
    a: direct democracy
    b: judicial review
    c: a separation of powers
    d: the supremacy of national laws over state laws

7. How many times does the word slavery or slaves appear in the original U.S. Constitution?
    a: none
    b: twice
    c: twenty
    d: two hundred and twenty

8. The first two opposing groups in U.S. politics were the:
    a: Republicans and Whigs
    b: Democrats and Republicans
    c: Federalists and Anti-Federalists
    d: Loyalists and Colonialists
    e: Cavaliers and Roundheads

9. The first form of the U.S. government was:
    a: anarchy, because of Shay's Rebellion
    b: the Bill of Rights
    c: the Constitution
    d: the Federalist Papers
    e: the Articles of Confederation

10. What was the purpose of the Federalist Papers?
    a: propaganda
    b: to create a political party
    c: to defend the Articles of Confederation
    d: to defend the U.S. Constitution

11. The United States of America is a:
    a: Rule of Law State
    b: Indirect (Representative) Democracy
    c: Constitutional Democracy
    d: Pimper's Paradise
    e: Direct Democracy

12. Identify the 3 plans proposed at the Constitutional Convention:

    a: limited govt., open govt., limited monarchy
    b: Ohio, Northwest Territory, Mason/Dixon
    c: New York, Georgia, Maryland
    d: Virginia, New Jersey, Connecticut
    e: New York, D.C., Virginia

13. Which state refused to send a delegation to the Constitutional Convention due to sympathy with Shay's Rebellion?

    a: New Hampshire   d: Massachusetts
    b: Rhode Island   e: Virginia
    c: Delaware

CHAPTER 4

Capitol Hill

Image © Alex Neauville, 2009. Used under license from Shutterstock, Inc.

Congress

There are significant differences between the House of Representatives and the Senate that remain largely unnoticed by the casual observer. By design, the House was the only body in our federal government that was popularly elected. Until the ratification of the 17th Amendment in 1913, senators were elected by state legislatures. Neither the President nor members of the federal judiciary are elected by the people. Therefore, it is the House that stood alone in upholding the concept of exemplifying the will of the people through duly elected representatives. The House has the power to impeach, but the Senate conducts the trial. The House has the power to choose the president in the event that no candidate gains a majority in the Electoral College, but the Senate must give advice and consent in the ratification of treaties, and in reference to presidential appointments. In modern America, a strong argument is noted for the House being the most democratic body. While it is true that senators are now popularly elected, the U.S. Senate hardly resembles the demographic makeup of today's society. For example, although 51% of the general population is female, they comprise only 20% of the U.S. Senate. The percentage is nearly the same in the House. Currently, only seventy-eight of the 435 members are women. It is therefore important not to be deceived by the fact that there are now more female members of Congress than at any time in American history, just as it is important not to be deceived by the fact that the President is an African American. Neither of these leadership positions indicates anything near proportional representation as related to gender or race. Overall, Congress is 82% male, and 84% white.

The House is also the chamber where every member is up for reelection every two years. This creates tremendous pressure on members to raise enough money to finance the increasingly costly campaigns for office. Moreover, senators need not be concerned about issues such as reapportionment, or redistricting as House members are. Reapportionment occurs every 10 years with whatever changes in population the Census reveals. This affects which states will receive what number of delegates to the House. Redistricting occurs as often as state legislatures deem it necessary, but usually coincides with Census results. This deals with how many congressional districts will exist within a state, and what the boundaries of those districts will be. Attendant with redistricting is the practice of gerrymandering, which is redrawing district boundaries to the advantage of a political party.

When one considers the need to raise funds, the possibilities of redistricting and reapportionment, and the committee system based on seniority, it is evident that House members must deal with distractions not visited upon members of the Senate. All of the above tend to push House members to proverbially "bring home the bacon" for their constituents as a means to maintain their status. Thus, the phenomenon of pork barreling. This is where members promote pet projects in their districts, even when those projects aid only a small proportion of constituents, increase the budget deficit, or strain the limits of fiscal discipline. As unseemly as this sounds, it works quite effectively. Constituents show their appreciation for the local federal projects either by voting for the member's reelection, contributing to the member's campaign, or both. In turn, incumbency has created an advantage that is difficult to overcome. Upwards of 85% of incumbents win reelection to Congress. Hence, as it pertains to the House, the founder's vision of turnover of membership through elections every two years is undermined by the aforementioned factors.

Leadership Positions

In the Senate there are several leadership positions with unique responsibilities. There are the Majority and Minority Leaders, the President Pro Tempore, and the Majority and Minority Whips. The Majority and Minority Leaders are the party spokespersons for their respective political parties. They set the agenda for their members. The President Pro Tempore presides over the Senate, and is usually the member from the majority party with the greatest seniority. The Majority and Minority Whips are responsible for counting votes among their members as specifically related to proposed legislation. The Whips also keep discipline among their members to vote the party line. Because the Senate has the deserved reputation of being more genteel than the House, rules are not as heavily emphasized. The most important rules in these legislative bodies are the rules of debate, because controlling debate is essential to controlling the pace and prospect for passage of legislation. The Senate has a longstanding tradition of open debate. In most instances, every member who wants to speak is given the opportunity to speak on the floor of the Senate to affirm or deny support for a bill.

Conversely, in the House there is no such tradition of open debate. In the House there are also several leadership positions. There are the House Majority and Minority Leaders. They do many of the same things as their counterparts in the Senate. There are also the House Majority and Minority Whips. However, the House has an extremely powerful position not found in the Senate. That position is second in line of succession to the presidency, and it is known as the Speaker of the House. Like the Senate Majority Leader, the Speaker of the House is a member of the majority party. However, unlike the Senate Majority Leader, the Speaker of the House enjoys unprecedented power over the legislative agenda in the House. The Speaker has at least seven discrete powers that shape what can occur in the House of Representatives. They are

1. The Speaker assigns bills to committees.
2. The Speaker can recognize members to speak in the House chamber.
3. The Speaker is the ultimate arbiter of the interpretation of House rules.
4. The Speaker appoints members to conference committees.
5. The Speaker assigns members to permanent committees.
6. The Speaker handpicks the nine members of the all-important Rules Committee.
7. The Speaker schedules votes in the full House on bills.

With this array of parliamentary weaponry in her or his arsenal, the Speaker's political power can rival that of the president. Within the structure of the House, the Speaker's determinations can make or break entire political careers. Those who show bright promise in the party can be elevated to sit on, or even to chair, the most influential committees. Those who fall into disfavor can find themselves lost in the political wilderness on a subcommittee for those with a limited political future.

It is important to recall that Congress is ruled by committee, and that the chair and majority of every committee are members of the majority party. Some of the most powerful committees (e.g., Rules or Appropriations) even have a supermajority of members from the dominant party. Also, of the four types of congressional committees, only standing committees can report legislation. Reporting legislation is necessary for a bill to be voted on.

Lastly, there is variance in the salaries of members and some leaders. Members of Congress are paid an annual salary of $174,000. Majority and Minority Leaders are paid an annual salary of $193,400. The Speaker of the House is paid an annual salary of $223,500.

How a Bill Becomes a Law

Congress has many functions, but its primary responsibility is to make laws that govern the nation. The process is an arduous one, and the life cycle of most bills is rather short. At numerous junctures in the process, a bill can die. Essentially, the process of legislative action is the same in both chambers of Congress. However, Article I, section 7, of the Constitution requires that all revenue bills originate in the House, although the Senate can amend those bills. This linkage of raising taxes is associated with the House because of its more democratic nature, and because of the strength of the foundational tenet of no taxation without representation.

Bills that are introduced into Congress usually come from one of three sources. They begin either as an idea from a member, from the President, or from lobbyists. Today, most of the ideas for bills come from lobbyists. In Washington, D.C., there is an area known as "K" street that is replete with a motley crew of peddlers of interest. A case in point is the circumstances surrounding the passage of a state bill that garnered national and international attention. In 2010 the Arizona state legislature passed a bill commonly known as SB 1070. Among other things, it sought to significantly toughen Arizona's treatment of those suspected of being illegal immigrants. The bill's initial sponsor was Arizona State Senator Russell Pearce.

In December 2009 Mr. Pearce met with other legislators, business interests, and lobbyists at the Grand Hyatt in Washington, D.C. This meeting location is a mere two city blocks from the aforementioned "K" street.

Mr. Pearce is a member of the task force of the American Legislative Exchange Council (ALEC). Within a matter of months, the bill had made its way to the Arizona statehouse floor, and two-thirds of the bill's co-sponsors were in attendance at the Grand Hyatt. There were also membership organizations like Reynolds American, Incorporated (tobacco industry); ExxonMobil (oil industry); National Rifle Association (NRA—gun industry); and the Corrections Corporation of America (CCA). The CCA is a billion dollar, largest private prison company in the country. Is it too much of a stretch that CCA perceived that tough state immigration measures like Arizona's SB 1070 would potentially fill their private prisons, ensuring increased profits? I think not.

According to a National Public Radio (NPR) broadcast I listened to, 30 of 36 of the co-sponsors for SB 1070 received donations from CCA and similar prison lobbyists/companies in the six months following the ALEC confab at the Grand Hyatt. Fortunately, in June 2012 the United States Supreme Court decision in *Arizona v. United States*, 567 U.S. _____ held that the most draconian aspects of SB 1070 were unconstitutional. Although this is an example of dealing with state legislation, the main point here is the undue influence of lobbies and lobbyists on the legislative process, whether it be a state or federal legislative effort. Far too many bills are conceived and written by lobbies and lobbyists.

Nonetheless, it takes a member to sponsor a bill in either chamber. Once the bill is introduced, if it is in the Senate, it is sent to the Majority Leader, and if it is the House, it is sent to the Speaker. The next step is for the bill to be assigned to a standing committee. This can result in nurturing or withering treatment for our young and vulnerable bill. The standing committee that the Congressional leader decides to send the bill to is a harbinger of its probability of becoming a successful piece of legislation. The bill is then reviewed by one of the several subcommittees attached to nearly each standing committee. There the bill will normally be subjected to amendments, hearings, investigations, and deliberations. The bill is then sent back in its new form to the standing committee, where more hearings and debate will likely occur. The term "markup" is applied if there is a final version of the bill that is sent to the full committee for a vote. If the markup is approved by a simple majority on the full committee, it will be reported out. This is where there is divergence between the House and the Senate.

In the Senate, the Majority Leader decides when to bring the bill to the floor of the Senate for debate. As stated, debate in the Senate is largely unlimited, and this subjects the bill to a possible filibuster. Once debate has ceased, the full Senate votes on the bill, and if it can obtain a simple majority of votes it passes.

In the House, once the bill is reported out of committee, it goes to the Rules Committee. The Rules Committee can then determine the parameters of the debate on the bill. The Rules Committee can issue a closed rule, which means that no amendments to the bill can be offered. Or, the Rules Committee can issue an open rule, which means that amendments can be allowed. This is an extremely crucial stage in how a bill becomes a law because an amendment can totally undermine the substance of the original bill. After the Rules Committee action, the bill is debated under the approved rules, and then submitted to a vote of the full House membership. If it passes by a simple majority vote, it has another hurdle to jump.

Once a bill passes both chambers, it is usually necessary to refine the differences in the two versions of the bill. The President can take action on only one document, therefore the bill is sent to the Conference Committee. The composition of the Conference Committee is determined by the House and Senate leadership. Most of the members of the Conference Committee are also members of the standing committee that performed the markup for the bill. If the differences in the two bills are resolved, the latest version is debated in both chambers. After the debate, each chamber votes, and if the bill passes by a simple majority vote in each chamber, it is sent to the President.

The President has four basic options when a bill arrives on her or his desk. The most frequent option exercised is for the President to sign the bill into law. The second option is to veto (Latin for "I forbid") the bill, and it does not become law, despite all the effort expended by Congress. Should this occur, Congress can override the veto, but this is exceedingly rare and difficult. In the entirety of American history, presidential vetoes have been overriden only 4% of the time. In order for Congress to override a presidential veto, it takes a supermajority vote of two-thirds of the members voting in each chamber. The third option is for the President to ignore the bill. If ten days elapse, and Congress is still in session, the bill automatically becomes a law. Lastly, the President can use what has come to be known as the "pocket veto." This is where the President ignores the bill, but Congress goes out of session. On the tenth day after the bill has arrived on the President's desk, it is rejected, and it does not become a law.

Hence, the life of a bill is a perilous one. At any one of the steps outlined above, a bill could die. In fact, the overwhelming majority of bills never make it out of full committee for floor debate or a floor vote. Moreover, for those bills that do eventually become law, many bear little resemblance to what their original sponsor(s) introduced. The name of the game in Congress is compromise. It is a system designed for incremental change. It is extraordinarily difficult to make significant change through the legislative process. The founders preferred it that way, but it is unclear whether the corruption that has plagued the process was given any consideration over two centuries ago.

However, when there is consensus, the slow, deliberative body known as Congress can act swiftly, sweepingly, and decisively. A case in point would be the passage of the USA PATRIOT Act in 2001. Within seven weeks after the heinous attacks of 11 September 2001, this Act was passed. Without a doubt, most members who voted for the Act (it passed both chambers overwhelmingly) never read the text, nor seriously considered its implications. Since its passage, significant portions of the USA PATRIOT Act have been deemed unconstitutional by the U.S. Supreme Court, or have not been renewed by Congress. The tendency in American history is to allow fear to subvert the legislative process under the inertia of becoming blatant reactionaries. Of course this would not be possible without the fiat of large swaths of the American public, but the pattern is quite disturbing. Another case in point is that the murderous year preceding 1964 created impetus for the passage of the Civil Rights and Voting Rights Acts that followed, but reaction rarely sustains the necessary stamina to prevail against huge challenges such as bigotry in all its shapes and forms. Therefore, even though good law can follow fleeting public distaste, a system so dependent on compromise is bound to crumble under the weight of diluted principles.

Enumerated Powers

Article I, section 8, of the U.S. Constitution contains over fifteen express powers of Congress. Among them are the power to tax, to borrow, to regulate commerce, to control citizenship and bankruptcies, to coin money, to establish patents and copyrights, to set up lower federal courts, to declare war, to create and organize a militia, and to create an army and navy. And, demonstrating some foresight, the founders did not restrict the powers of Congress to an exhaustive list. The necessary and proper clause serves to give pause to the strict constructionist argument about constitutional interpretation. Because the enumerated powers are capped with the flexibility of having the power to make laws that were not foreseeable at the ratification of the instrument, Congress has remained vital and relevant.

Elastic Clause

Also known as the necessary and proper clause, this power constitutionally granted to Congress is the political equivalent of a catchall. Simply put, Congress can make whatever laws it deems that it must, in order to effect the enumerated powers. In the 1819 landmark case *McCulloch v. Maryland,* the U.S. Supreme Court linked the enumerated power to tax and spend with the creation of a Second Bank of the United States. When the state of Maryland attempted to tax the bank, it was held unconstitutional. This meant that an implied power of Congress could be used to protect an expressed power of Congress. Thus, in the early decades of the Republic, the federal government carved out its supremacy over states. It is now accepted that states have no ability to tax the federal government.

Commerce Clause

Revisiting this enumerated power is important as a point of emphasis, because the power of Congress to regulate interstate commerce is the most widely interpreted clause of the U.S. Constitution. The seminal case here is the 1824 Supreme Court holding in *Gibbons v. Ogden.* The significance of the case is the broad interpretation of interstate commerce. It is not as important to know that the case dealt with invalidating a New York law as it is to know that navigation was defined as a part of interstate commerce. Since this case, the Supreme Court has undulated in its interpretation of the breadth of the Commerce Clause. For a large part of the remainder of the 19th Century, the Court gave a broad interpretation of the power to regulate under the Commerce Clause. Then, during the first four decades of the 20th Century, the Court tightened its interpretation of the scope of the Commerce Clause. This view prevailed until the "switch in time that saved nine" of the New Deal era. Yet, an "about face" was taken by the Court in the holdings of the 1995 case of *United States v. Lopez,* and the 2000 case of *United States v. Morrison.* In both of those cases, the Court adopted a limiting view of Congress's power to legislate using the Commerce Clause. This was the first time that the Court took that position since before the New Deal. However, this all changed in 2005, with the Rehnquist Court's majority decision in *Gonzales v. Raich.* In that case, the Court flip-flopped by holding that there was an appropriate use of the Commerce Clause, even though there was no interstate commerce involved. The case arose in Butte County, California, and it challenged a federal law criminalizing marijuana. This ruling ignored the fact that the marijuana in question was home-grown in California, was consumed in California, was never transported or sold across state borders, and was given legal sanction under California's Medical Marijuana law. It seems that if you carry a concealed gun in a school zone (*Lopez*), or beat a woman in a domestic dispute (*Morrison*), the Court will not allow Congress to intervene, but if you smoke a reefer for your health in a state that says it is legal to do so, the Court will not protect you from the reach of Congress's power. Quoting from the dissent in the *Gonzales* case: "Respondents Diane Monson and Angel Raich use marijuana that has never been bought or sold, that has never crossed state lines, and that has had no demonstrable effect on the national market for marijuana. If Congress can regulate this under the Commerce Clause, then it can regulate virtually anything—and the federal Government is no longer one of limited and enumerated powers." It is more than fair to say that there appears to be an inconsistency in the current scope of the Commerce Clause. A possible explanation could be the complexity of the interrelationship between state and federal law.

There is a doctrine in the law known as *preemption*. This is where conflict between state and federal law is resolved in favor of federal law under the Supremacy Clause of the U.S. Constitution, Article VI, section 2. However, preemption should not be confused with challenges to the constitutionality of federal law. Preemption relates only to federalism as a matter of power-sharing between the states and the federal government. An interesting case in point about constitutionality and federal law is the 1996 Defense of Marriage Act.

Defense of Marriage Act

The Defense of Marriage Act (hereinafter known as DOMA) is a curious case in federalism because it touches upon constitutional areas such as the Article IV, section 1, Full Faith and Credit Clause, and the Due Process and Equal Protection Clauses of the Fourteenth Amendment. There is a history of Congress passing laws that were later deemed unconstitutional in whole or part. One of the most glaring examples is the Alien and Sedition Acts passed in 1798. The greatest contemporary relevance of these Acts is the fact that, although three of the four Acts have long been expired or been repealed, the Alien Enemies Act is still enforceable law. In fact, it is codified as United States Code, Title 50, Chapter 3, sections 21–24. These laws give the President the authority to apprehend and deport resident aliens whose home countries are at war with the United States. But, the law requires that the war be declared against a foreign nation or government, so its use as a tool in the War on Terror is dubious at best. And, its use to place nearly 120,000 people of Japanese descent in concentration camps during World War II is troubling, especially taking into account that two-thirds of those interned were American citizens.

Returning to DOMA, is it possible that America is currently tolerating Congress having passed an unconstitutional law? Is the reading of Article IV, section 1, "Congress may by general laws prescribe the Manner in which such Acts, Records, and Proceedings be proved, and the Effect thereof," sufficient to ban federal recognition of state laws that allow same sex marriage? Until May 2009, President Obama supported repeal of DOMA. But in court proceedings challenging the constitutionality of DOMA, President Obama's Justice Department filed a brief defending DOMA. Only one as skilled in rhetoric as President Obama would have the temerity to simultaneously call for Congressional repeal of the law, while at the same time defending it as preserving long-standing state authority to define marriage, and saving taxpayer dollars. One wonders if the quite similar arguments against interracial marriage strike the President as ironic, considering the fact that his parents were an interracial couple who married in Hawaii prior to the Supreme Court decision striking down bans on interracial marriages in *Loving v. Virginia* (1967). For years the Supreme Court had been successful in dodging this important, yet divisive issue. There had been several requests for a writ of certiorari, before the Court finally accepted a case for review. Greater detail of DOMA will be provided in Chapter 6 of this text.

Senate Confirmation

Another extremely important area of Congressional oversight is the role and duty of the Senate to provide advice and consent on the President's judicial appointments. Of particular interest was the first opportunity for President Obama to fill a vacant position on the Supreme Court. His nominee was the first Latina to be a Chief Executive's choice for the highest court in the land. The Senate's power to confirm or deny judicial appointments is undoubtedly its highest-profile moments outside of the rarity of a presidential impeachment trial. But beyond the drama and spectacle is the all important shaping of the federal judiciary as a facilitator of policy change. Today, there is a near even split of the sitting federal judges appointed by presidents. This includes Judge Sonia Sotomayor, who was initially appointed to the federal bench by Republican President George H.W. Bush.

With the strong majority enjoyed by Democrats in the Senate, Judge Sotomayor's confirmation was hardly in doubt. We have already witnessed the difficulty her nomination creates for Republicans. Desperately needing to broaden the appeal of their party in disarray, but unwilling to become more inclusive, Republicans have already blundered by allowing reckless and damaging vitriol to characterize Judge Sotomayor. She has been called a racist for her pronouncement of her view of combining her background with her responsibilities as a jurist. It is unimaginable how such aspersions could be helpful to the Republican Party with such an important and growing demographic segment as Latinos. The national election results of the 2010 and 2012 elections are clear evidence of inept, ideologically inert Republican politics. What remains an intriguing question (particularly after his second nomination of a woman to the Court— Elena Kagan) is whether President Obama will get another, or other, chances to nominate members to the Supreme Court. If so, there is a real prospect of a sea change afoot in the judicial branch of our federal government. The strong Latino support enjoyed by the President in the last election cycle (they voted 71% for Obama) should have jolted the Republican Party to change tack, but the current developments in the debate on Immigration Reform would seem to conjure up the electoral message having been "lost in translation."

Immigration Reform

Most controversial issues in American politics lack the clarity that exists with the need to take action on illegal immigration. Regardless of political leanings, an overwhelming majority of Americans realize that something substantial must be done to tackle this problem. The assessment of why it is a problem varies widely, but the fact that it is a problem is nearly universally accepted. In 1986 Congress passed a bill that was signed into law by then President Ronald Reagan. At that time there were approximately 3 million undocumented aliens in this country, and the law offered amnesty to them. Nearly 30 years later this country is saddled with an undocumented population that ranges between 11 and 12 million people. That number would probably be larger had it not been for the economic meltdown of 2008.

In July 2013 there seems to be some traction on passing an immigration reform bill. On 27 June 2013 the Senate acted, passing SB 744 by a 68 to 32 margin. Fourteen Republicans voted with the 52 Democrats and 2 Independents. Now it is up to the House. The Senate version of immigration reform included provisions that will be difficult to find approval among many House Republicans. The most onerous to Republicans is the pathway to citizenship. Other provisions are: a national employment eligibility verification scheme, a temporary worker program, and increased visa allowances for skilled foreign workers.

What is not at all clear is where Republicans stand on immigration reform. The Republican Party leadership realizes that it is political suicide not to act, but the rank and file members are greatly divided. The House members' insistence on alienating (pun intended) border control measures as a precursor to even allow the bill to the House floor portends a lack of understanding of how pressing most Americans view immigration reform. More importantly, the Republican Party leadership understands the erosion for support if the GOP continues to rely on an aging and diminishing white population that is not inclusive. The "browning" of America is occurring before our very eyes. The most populous state in the Union (California) is already a minority-majority state. More than half of the babies born in the U.S. are people of color. Within 40 years whites will be just another minority group in this country. Nevertheless, the Republican Party is in the throes of ideologues who simultaneously help and hurt their cause. The Tea Party and Conservative Christians help the GOP as a galvanized base. But, the Tea Party and Conservative Christians hurt the GOP as being so ideologically driven that compromise and bipartisan efforts are equated with something akin to treason. One can't help but wonder if the feeble efforts of outreach to Latinos by Republicans is borne of sincerity, or petty politics. On the one hand, Republicans know they need to broaden their appeal or be relegated to a regional (as opposed to national) party. On the other hand, allowing undocumented aliens to become citizens also means allowing them to become voters. With vitriolic and racist pronouncements from some members to the GOP, the damage could already be done. In that event, the fear factor of creating more voters who support Democrat party candidates is too risky for those whose tendency is to be rather resistant to change. Bold initiative, which is what serious immigration reform requires, is not the province of today's Republicans. Even if the leaders of the GOP recognize the necessity of bipartisan action, they risk falling out of favor with their base constituents. Speaker of the House John Boehner is a perfect example. Can he truly risk allowing the Senate version of immigration reform to be brought to the House floor for a vote? What if it passes with overwhelming Democrat support, and a small percentage of Republican support? This is what happened in the Senate, but the Senate is controlled by Democrats. Could the Speaker maintain his leadership position, or in this poisonous atmosphere would he be labeled a traitor? The latter is most likely.

In the meantime, Republicans seem to be content with merely recruiting Latino candidates for key offices, but this isn't working so well. Within the last months Republicans were unable to capture the Massachusetts Senate seat vacated when Democrat John Kerry became Secretary of State. In a special election Republicans presented a rather attractive Latino candidate. Even though he was a political newcomer, Gabriel Gomez had attributes and a circumstance that you might think would assure his election. A former Navy SEAL and investment banker, he lost to veteran politician Ed Markey, himself a flawed candidate. It appears that Markey's victory was more the result of the Republicans' lack of being able to harness the enthusiasm of the Tea Party wing than the fact that Massachusetts is a Democrat stronghold, and Markey was heavily support by the Democrat party machine.

The real point here is that the moderation it takes to support immigration reform is alienating to the non centrist, ideologically fringe element that is the core of the Tea Party, which is the most galvanizing camp among Republicans. The ideological shift necessary will not be forthcoming anytime soon.

Campaign Finance Reform

The democratic process of electing officials is at the heart of the integrity of a society that claims to be based on equality. The notion of "one person, one vote" as enunciated in the 1964 United States Supreme Court decision *Reynolds v. Sims,* 377 U.S. 533 is at great risk. In 2010 the United State Supreme Court decision *Citizens United v. Federal Election Commission,* 558 U.S. 310 basically eviscerated the sanctity of the principle of "one person, one vote." This is the contention because the holding in *Citizens* equates money with free speech. If one has more money, then one has more free speech. When this is applied to the financing of political campaigns for public office, there can be no legitimate claim to the equality principle in "one person, one vote." It is no surprise that the average cost of a campaign to become elected to the House of Representatives now nears two million dollars. The average cost of a campaign to become elected to the United States Senate now nears ten million dollars. Of course, in many states those costs are more than doubled. In order to have a chance to win election to the White House, a candidate must be prepared to spend nearly a billion dollars.

The demands of raising so much money to win election to the federal government are political, moral, and social corruption. For the past forty years or so Congress has passed legislation to thwart the negative influence of money on the democratic electoral process. Beginning in 1971 with the Federal Election Campaign Act (and the 1974 amendments), the constitutionality thereof was upheld by the United States Supreme Court in the 1976 decision in *Buckley v. Valeo,* 424 U.S. 1. Again, in 2002 Congress took action with the passage of the Bipartisan Campaign Reform Act (also known as "McCain/Feingold." And once again the constitutionality thereof was upheld by the United States Supreme Court in the *McConnell v. Federal Election Commission,* 540 U.S. 93. But these legislative efforts at campaign finance reform were given a devastating blow by the Court's decision in *Citizens United.* The violence done to the principle of electoral equality has its genesis in capitalism. It is long established in American jurisprudence that corporations are seen as persons in the eyes of the law. Only in an economic system where profit exceeds the importance of people could the rights that people enjoy be shared with an entity as inanimate as a corporation.

Of the fifty states of the United States only three (Arizona, Connecticut, and Maine) have fully publicly financed elections. Unfortunately, just as the efforts of Congress have fallen woefully short, so have the state schemes. For one thing, the public financing is not mandatory. In a more perfect union, all elections in the United States would be publicly financed. There is probably not a better use of taxpayer dollars than to rid the system of the inevitable corruption that a free flow of money brings. What I propose is that in every election in this country that a threshold number of signatures via petition place a candidate on the ballot. My suggestion is that the number of verified signatures should be a percentage of the voters in a previous election cycle. Once the list of qualified candidates is established they are allocated the same amount of campaign funds. The qualified candidates can spend the funds (legally) in whatever manner suits them. It is my prediction that the results of this sort of campaign finance reform will be:

1. the reduction and perhaps elimination of financial corruption in the election process;
2. the increase of transparency in the electoral process;
3. the breaking of the stranglehold of the two party system; and
4. the increase of political participation in the electoral system of common citizens.

These results would tremendously strengthen our democracy, and most likely lead to a more representative, and relevant governance. This proposal has little chance in our current political climate. Big monied interests are choking the life out of the democratic process today, and the less than 10% approval rating of Congress speaks volumes for the negative effect of the cancerous corruption afflicting our governmental institutions. It will take a changing of the make-up of the United States Supreme Court for this sort of reform to have any opportunity to prevail.

Overview

The design of Congress was for slow and tedious proceedings that bend toward failure of reaching the original objective. The institutional protection of the status quo can hardly be overstated. This makes total sense if your reflection includes a robust knowledge and understanding of American history. But, most Americans are neither reflective nor knowledgeable about the workings of the federal legislature. A telling by-product of the emphasis on rugged individualism is a self-centeredness that is justifiable only if ideologically attached to human nature itself. Whether this characterization of human nature is true or not is not important in contemporary America.

For example, many Americans thoughtlessly support greater punishment as a remedy for crime, but few support attacking poverty and/or the lack of a high-quality education. This is besides the undeniably strong correlations between poverty, low-quality schooling, and criminal behavior. Many Americans are repulsed by senseless acts of violence using firearms, but few support Congressional action on reasonable gun control. This is even after too many shooting tragedies to recall. If there is no will to do anything after children are murdered like what happened in December 2012 at Sandy Hook Elementary in Newtown, Connecticut, cynicism takes firm hold. No wonder that the public approval rating of Congress is at an all time low of 9%, and the public disapproval of Congress hovers at a celestial 85%. Many Americans claim to be Christians, yet support capital punishment. Many Americans decry bigotry, yet are racist themselves. Many Americans claim to believe in equality, but not for those who choose to love and marry within the same gender. Hence, the continuation of fundamental contradictions dogs our past, our present, and most likely our future. The Defense of Marriage Act was chosen as a Congressional example of discrimination supported by our government. One can't help but wonder whether the institution of marriage can be defended by the throngs of divorced heterosexuals in this country. Or, whether either major party can be trusted to make the prospect of prosperity brighter for the coming generations. This sentiment and unease is empirically substantiated by any number of recent polls. Obviously, there has been a rise with the onset of the Obama Administration and its efforts to stop the freefalling economy, but it is safe to say that Congress has a way to go to reinstill faith in its capacity to serve the needs of its constituent American people.

The disillusionment has caused a dangerous fraying of civility. Increasing numbers of Americans view their government as the problem. In some cases citizens actually view government as the enemy. This is particularly incendiary, given the availability of propaganda on the Internet. There have undoubtedly always been fringe elements in this society, but in prior times they remained relatively isolated. The blogosphere allows baseless claims to catch like wildfire. Just feeling that there are others who share your warped view of the world is a great impetus for holding fast to that which could otherwise be quickly dismissed as ludicrous. A recent example is the so-called "birther movement" that seeks to convince the unwitting that President Obama is not an American citizen, and is therefore unqualified to hold the highest office in the land. One need only search the public records of Hawaii to view his birth certificate, but some choose to accept Obama's political rise as some sort of Antichrist evil plot. As ridiculous as it may seem, there are far too many Americans who view the ineptitude in both chambers of Congress, coupled with a Democrat President who happens to be an African American with an Islamic name, as the end of all days. When mixed with the tenuous economic climate, hate speech parading on talk radio as gospel, and a broader culture that is morally bankrupt, America is one catastrophe away from something akin to chaos. Historically, Congress has not been ahead of such rumblings. Every significant social movement in the United States has been chased by Congress, not lead by it. This includes the abolition of slavery, women's suffrage, the Labor Movement, the Civil Rights Movement, the Antiwar Movement, the Women's Rights Movement, and the Gay Rights Movement.

Chapter 4
Study Guide

1. How many senators does it take to invoke cloture?

   a: 5   d: 49

   b: 60   e: 51

   c: 100

2. Does the "Bradley Effect" help or hurt Black candidates for public office?

   a: it helps   b: it hurts

3. Does the "Reverse Bradley Effect" help or hurt Black candidates for public office?

   a: it helps   b: it hurts

4. Identify the correct number of members needed to override a presidential veto in the House and Senate (respectively):

   a: 435/100   c: 218/51

   b: 535/100   d: 291/67

5. Interest groups are broken into the following categories except:

   a: demographic groups   c: single-issue groups

   b: bigots   d: public interest groups

6. Although people do not have much confidence in government institutions, polls show that they:

   a: expect government to solve major problems

   b: expect nonprofits to solve major problems

   c: expect individuals to solve major problems by dropping out of society

   d: avoid thinking about problems

7. The most important influence on political socialization is:

   a: peer group   d: video games

   b: family   e: education

   c: political events

8. The aggregate of individual attitudes or beliefs shared by some portion of adults is referred to as:

   a: political opinion   c: public opinion
   b: propaganda   d: an ideology

9. The theory that views politics as a struggle among interest groups is

_____.

   a: bipolarism   c: democracy
   b: pluralism– *a condition/system*   d: elitism
          in which 2+ more states/group/ coexist.

10. What is the nation's largest interest group?

   a: AARP   c: NAZI
   b: NAACP   d: NRA

11. Interest groups tend to have a _____ bias.

   a: lower class   c: ethnic
   b: racial   d: middle- to upper-class

12. Which of the following *is not* one of the main techniques used by interest groups?

   a: rioting
   b: lobbying
   c: ratings of legislative behavior
   d: campaign assistance

13. Interest groups are often spawned by mass:

   a: media   c: social movements
   b: hysteria   d: spectrometer

14. A situation in which one major party controls the presidency and the other controls Congress is referred to as _____ _____.

   a: problematic   c: divided government
   b: a balance of power   d: good government

15. How can Congress check/balance the President?

   a: through lobbying
   b: through the veto override
   c: through using the bully pulpit
   d: Congress can not

16. The best indication that political parties have weakened in the last three decades is:

    a: they're not the show they used to be
    b: the election of Barack Obama
    c: the divorce rate
    d: Florida 2000
    e: low party identification

17. Discrimination in most housing was forbidden by the:

    a: Civil Rights Act of 1870
    b: Voting Rights Act of 1965
    c: Civil Rights Act of 1964
    d: Equal Housing Act of 1965
    e: Civil Rights Act of 1968

18. The lecture on Public Opinion included the following information on polling and statistics except:

    a: representative samples
    b: random samples
    c: free samples
    d: telephone surveys
    e: margin of error

19. This is the only state that has completely abandoned physical precinct polling places:

    a: Hawaii
    b: Missouri
    c: Puerto Rico
    d: Maine
    e: Oregon

20. This man is most closely identified with Public Interest Groups:

    a: Andrew Jackson
    b: Ralph Nader
    c: Ralph Cramden
    d: Ralph Bunche
    e: Andrew Johnson

21. Today, a person with only a high school education is more likely to vote for a candidate from which major political party?

    a: Republican
    b: Green
    c: Libertarian
    d: Democrat
    e: Peace and Freedom

22. Today, a person with a postgraduate education is more likely to vote for a candidate from which major political party?

    a: Republican
    b: Green
    c: Libertarian
    d: Democrat
    e: Peace and Freedom

23. Which statement is correct with respect to age as a factor in voting?
    a: age is not a significant factor in voting
    b: younger voters tend to turn out in higher percentages than older voters
    c: turnout increases the older the age groups until the age of 65 and older
    d: younger voters have more enthusiasm for voting than older voters

24. As a factor in voting, more education seems to be correlated with voting _____.
    a: Democratic   c: Green
    b: Republican   d: Libertarian

25. Extension of the franchise to Black males occurred with the passage of the _____ Amendment in 1870.
    a: 15th   c: 17th
    b: 16th   d: 18th

26. The Senate is the chamber of the Congress that:
    a: must first approve all money bills
    b: must first approve amendments
    c: ratifies treaties
    d: has the first opportunity to override presidential vetoes

27. Some functions are restricted to only one house of Congress. The Senate is the only house that can:
    a: propose amendments
    b: approve presidential appointments
    c: approve the budget
    d: investigate the president

28. The *central* difference between the House and the Senate is that the:
    a: House is much larger in membership than the Senate
    b: House represents people, the Senate represents geography
    c: Senate first appropriates money
    d: House first appropriates money

29. For the House of Representatives:
   - a: each state is allowed at least one representative
   - b: there is no set number of minimum or maximum for each state
   - c: each state is allowed two representatives
   - d: membership for each state is determined by the House itself

30. Midterm Congressional elections:
   - a: usually result in the president's party losing seats in Congress
   - b: attract more voters than presidential elections
   - c: attract as many voters as presidential elections
   - d: usually result in the president's party gaining seats in Congress

31. Gerrymandering refers to the process of:
   - a: ending debate in the Senate
   - b: redrawing legislative boundaries
   - c: forcing a bill out of committee
   - d: selecting a committee chair

32. In the House of Representatives, the majority leader:
   - a: acts as the spokesperson for the majority party in the House
   - b: serves as Speaker of the House
   - c: is elected in a vote of all members of the House
   - d: is rarely able to exert any meaningful leadership because of the dominance of the Speaker

33. The fiscal year (FY) of the federal government is:
   - a: January to December
   - b: April to February
   - c: October to September
   - d: July to June

34. What is the ultimate check that Congress has over the bureaucracy?
   - a: the blank check
   - b: withholding the appropriations of money
   - c: the rubber check
   - d: the pocket veto

35. How huge is the current approximate U.S. national debt?
   - a: $2 trillion
   - b: $25 trillion
   - c: $17 trillion
   - d: $200 billion
   - e: $5.6 trillion

36. Why did Congress create agencies within the federal bureaucracy?
    - a: to implement federal legislation
    - b: to implement state legislation
    - c: to stop government corruption
    - d: to create a system of patronage

37. In order to change the U.S. Constitution, either Congress or the state conventions must have this fraction voting in favor (respectively):
    - a: 3/5 & 7/8
    - b: 2/3 & 3/4
    - c: 3/5 & 1/2
    - d: 1/3 & 5/6

38. Sunset legislation refers to:
    - a: the use of the pocket veto
    - b: the idea of automatic program termination after a prescribed period unless Congress reauthorizes it
    - c: environmental protection laws
    - d: safe transportation laws

39. An unfunded mandate is:
    - a: the same as porkbarreling
    - b: the same as gerrymandering
    - c: when the federal government doesn't provide money to carry out a policy
    - d: when a social event is ruined by a cheapskate

40. Senate Rule 22 refers to the closing of debate and:
    - a: judicial appointments
    - b: the "nuclear option"
    - c: cloak and dagger
    - d: majority rule
    - e: filibustering

41. The term "suffrage" refers to:
    - a: the miseries that come from being unable to vote
    - b: the right to vote
    - c: paying poll taxes
    - d: the right to hold public office

42. The term "turnout" describes the number of people who:
    - a: register to vote
    - b: actually vote
    - c: vote for the incumbent
    - d: a & b

43. The phenomenon called the "gender gap" refers to the fact that:

   a: more women vote for Democrats than do men
   b: more men vote than do women
   c: in families, it is usually women who determine how the family votes
   d: more men than women have had their ballot invalidated

44. What changed the Black allegiance from the Republican to the Democrat party?

   a: the New Deal   d: Abraham Lincoln
   b: Andrew Johnson   e: the Raw Deal
   c: the Square Deal

45. The network of policy making that includes congressional committees is called the:

   a: issue network   c: iron triangle
   b: internetwork   d: social movements

46. Which of the following political parties was the precursor to the Republican party?

   a: Tories   d: KKK
   b: Libertarians   e: Federalists
   c: Whigs

47. What is a "free rider"?

   a: a freeloader
   b: a beneficiary
   c: pro bono legal representation
   d: a beneficiary who doesn't contribute

48. This 1976 Supreme Court case declared it unconstitutional for Congress to limit the amount of money that an individual candidate could spend on her or his own behalf:

   a: *Buckley v. Valeo*   c: *Plessy v. Ferguson*
   b: *U.S. v. Nixon*   d: *Dred Scott v. Sandford*

49. According to lecture, the difference between reapportionment and redistricting is:

    a: one relates to Congress, and the other relates to states
    b: there is no difference
    c: one relates to the House, and the other to the Senate
    d: one is a constant, and the other is a variable

50. Select the factual combination of current "party control" of the 3 branches of the federal government:

    a: Congress = Repub., Executive = Repub., Supreme Court = Demo.
    b: Congress = Repub., Executive = Repub., Supreme Court = Repub.
    c: Congress = Demo., Executive = split, Supreme Court = Demo.
    d: Congress = Demo., Executive = Repub., Supreme Court = Repub.
    e: Congress = split, Executive = Demo., Supreme Court = Repub.

51. What percentage of today's electorate are registered as independent voters?

    a: 100%   d: 33%
    b: 50%   e: 75%
    c: 42%

52. Select the factual combination of the (2013) 113th Congress:

    a: House = Repub., Senate = Repub.
    b: House = Repub., Senate = Demo.
    c: House = Demo., Senate = Repub.
    d: House = Demo., Senate = Demo.

53. According to Chapter 4 of the Tarikh text, Congress is:

    a: a great institution
    b: 82% male, 84% white
    c: 48% male, 86% white
    d: out of touch with the American people

CHAPTER 5

The Oval Office

Image © Mary Ann Madsen, 2009. Used under license from Shutterstock, Inc.

Leadership

Of all the positions in the federal government, the Presidency is the most recognizable. If one were to ask the average American who their Congressional representatives were, or were to show the same person a photo image of any of them, it is not very likely that most citizens could identify their leaders. But, it is a wholly different matter when speaking of the President of the United States. In fact, most adults on this planet could identify the President, and billions would ascribe the title of "leader of the free world" to her or him. This high profile has benefits and detriments that are closely linked to each other. Beneficially, a mere announcement or declaration from the President is a newsworthy event that can catapult a backburner issue directly to the forefront of American or world priorities. Detrimentally, any time that the President misspeaks could cause grave consequences, sometimes even resulting in death.

Therefore, the President has to constantly walk a tightrope of utterances. What is required is a balancing act, and nowhere is this more evident or have a greater impact than in the realm of foreign policy. It would seem that every President wants to leave some sort of legacy. As counterintuitive as it may sound, in these modern times, it is easier to craft a legacy on foreign policy, than to craft domestic policy. The fact that we live in an interdependent, global economy is very important. The ability of a president to craft foreign policy is much broader than her or his ability to craft domestic policy. Much of this is due to tradition and the U.S. Constitution, but as long as Congress does not meet its duty to provide a check and a balance to the activity of the Executive branch, this will continue to be the case. For example, the mindless following of an ill-conceived and overly belligerent foreign policy under the administration of George W. Bush resulted in the current quagmires of Iraq and Afghanistan. It took several years for the Supreme Court to repudiate that administration's handling of captured "terrorists." One must be reminded that Congress has control of the almighty federal purse strings.

This is not to say that Congress is stymied only when it comes to foreign matters. Today, few believe that responsibility for our current economic crisis can be laid solely at the doorstep of 1600 Pennsylvania Avenue. Congress repeatedly failed to regulate markets and curb spending, while passing legislation that included tax cuts for the wealthiest members of our society. Meanwhile, the Supreme Court was directly responsible for the George W. Bush Administration ever coming into being. The point is that the abdication of fulfilling their duties of checking and balancing the power of the Executive is more understandable when it comes to foreign as opposed to domestic policy. It is within the purview of the President to set the foreign policy agendas for this country. This is particularly evident in our dealings with Iran, Israel, North Korea, and Pakistan. Although the Obama Administration has exchanged the foolhardy sabre rattling of the G. W. Bush Administration (with its bellicose recriminations about an "axis of evil" and the like) with a more measured approach, and less less hyperbolic rhetoric, it has been significantly more aggressive with the use of drone aircraft to fight the "War on Terror". No Congressional or Supreme Court support is necessary, although having Congressional support for foreign policy is greatly helpful.

Bully Pulpit

Whether it be a domestic or foreign issue, the President enjoys unprecedented influence when it comes to shaping the federal agenda and public opinion. Most of the press conferences and addresses to the nation by the President are covered in real time. Only recently have there been grumblings from network executives about the loss of revenue during presidential media events. This loss of revenue is due to the fact that there are no commercial breaks during press conferences, or addresses, to the nation. It is those commercial breaks in coverage that provide money to television outlets. Without those advertisements, and the revenues they generate, television outlets operate at a financial loss by covering commercial-free presidential events. This provides a sort of built-in curb on presidential abuse of the bully pulpit. The President has to be careful not to saturate the marketplace of ideas by being too repetitive with a political message or position. Nonetheless, the utilization of various media by the President to garner support is an effective use of the most powerful position in the world.

Commander-in-Chief

Just as it is true that the Office of the President is the most recognizable in our federal government, so is the role of Commander-in-Chief. This unquestionable executive power is specifically enunciated in Article II of the U.S. Constitution. Nonetheless, the role of Commander-in-Chief of the U.S. Armed Forces is not without controversy. A key question is what power does the Commander-in-Chief have, and what limits are placed on that power in terms of the prosecution of war? This serious dilemma has been made more difficult to resolve because Congress has not declared war in over sixty years.

Because of the abuses of power that domestically involved the Federal Bureau of Investigation (FBI) and its Counter Intelligence Program (COINTELPRO), and in foreign affairs involved the undeclared war in Southeast Asia, Congress decided to take action. In 1973, Congress overrode President Nixon's veto and passed the War Powers Act. This Act required the President to notify Congress and obtain its approval if American troops were sent into hostilities for more than sixty days. It placed a limit on the use of American troops at ninety days, after which either a use-of-force resolution or a declaration of war was mandated. It must be noted that every President since its passage has declared it unconstitutional. This is despite the fact that the U.S. Supreme Court has been accorded the function of being the final arbiter on what is, or is not constitutional. After the Vietnam War was exposed for the debacle that it was, it is understandable that Congress would attempt to wrest back its constitutional authority to declare war. This became imperative after the pattern of American military failures had taken shape. There was the undeclared Korean War, the Bay of Pigs fiasco, and then the pretextual and fabricated Gulf of Tonkin incident. Since its passage, the War Powers Act has been a rather toothless tiger. Again, Congress has not declared war, but American presidents have sent troops to such places as Lebanon, Grenada, Panama, Haiti, Somalia, Kosovo, Iraq, Afghanistan, and so forth.

Drone Usage to Kill American Citizens

Notwithstanding the harshness of this charge, the Obama Administration has embarked down a pathway of criminality that echoes the excesses of the Nixon Administration. At least partially due to a lack of an alternative, President Obama is more than content alienating his base of supporters. He has done this through a number of initiatives, but the focus here is on the targeting of American citizens for extrajudicial murder. It remains unclear what the legal justification is. Attorney General Eric Holder has attempted to articulate a legal basis for these assassinations, but he has come up way short of a justification. The unwillingness to reveal not only who is on this target list, or why an American is on this target list will continue to erode the public's confidence and belief in the rule of law. Even if the approach of extrajudicial killings did not include Americans, the justification would be dubious. This begs the question of where the line is drawn. Thus far, what the government has revealed about these killings have involved actions abroad. However, reviewing Attorney General Holder's contentions, there would seem to be no territorial limit to these murders. It would seem that the strongest defense of this approach is the imminence of the threat to the United States. But, how imminent can the threat be if the murders are occurring far from American shores? And, according to a Justice Department "white paper," Attorney General Holder and Central Intelligence Agency (CIA) Director Brennan have a greatly expanded concept of what imminent means. Vague terminology like "recently" or "activities" have been used as a basis to assert the legality of these targeted murders of American citizens. A failure to renounce or disavow threatening "activities" is apparently now the standard to "greenlight" these killings. As a reminder, our federal government is clearly restrained from violations of due process by the 5th Amendment to the U.S. Constitution. Such a pointed critique demands a convincing example.

Anwar al-Awlaki, Samir Khan, and Abdulrahman al-Awlaki were all American citizens. Both of the al-Awlakis (father and son) were born on American soil. Samir Khan was not. He is of Pakistani descent, born in Saudi Arabia, and raised in New York. Anwar al-Awlaki was born in Las Cruces, New Mexico, and his son Abdulrahman was born in Denver, Colorado. At the time of the younger al-Awlaki's death he was a mere 16 years old. Each of them were murdered without charges nor trial by the American government in the country of Yemen. The United States is not at war with Yemen. The CIA made its first known attempt on the life of Anwar al-Awlaki on 5 May 2011 in Yemen by way of a failed drone attack. The CIA was successful in assassinating Anwar al-Awlaki and Samir Khan in the same drone attack on 30 September 2011 in northern Yemen. At the time of their murders, neither men were directly engaged in activity that could in any way be interpreted to pose an imminent threat to the United States, or any American.

Due to U.S. governmental excesses in the 1960s (compare the unlawful murder of any number of members of the Black Panther Party) and the 1970s (CIA assassinations of any number of foreign political figures), then President Gerald Ford issued Executive Order 11905 in 1976. Consequently, then President Jimmy Carter issued Executive Order 12036 in 1978. Both Executive Orders sought to prohibit the U.S. government from participating in assassinations. In fact, Executive Order 12036 expanded the prohibition to anyone associated with the U.S. government. Additionally, federal law prohibits the killing of Americans on foreign soil. Section 1119 of 18 Chapter United States Code (U.S.C.) is even titled "Foreign Murder of United States Nationals."

As the reader of this text, a challenge is being presented to you. Are your critical thinking skills well enough developed to understand that when Americans engage in conduct that is threatening, treasonous, or harmful to the Republic that as a matter of the rule of law they should be formally charged, and brought to a fair trial? Is it too daunting to live by the creed and code that is outlined in the U.S. Constitution? Because when we do not, or we allow our leaders to secretly engage in murderous behavior civil society is at great risk. The Obama Administration has yet to fully explain why an American child was murdered on foreign soil by government forces just two weeks after his father was murdered by those same forces. Is the killing of Abdulrahman al-Awlaki a "mistake," or is the entire approach a mistake?

Some years ago the term "Imperial Presidency" was coined to describe the ever increasing reach for power by the Executive branch. Where is the counterbalance that is the design of the Madisonian Model? President Obama may be characterized by many as soft on terrorists, but nothing could be farther from the truth. Senator Obama may have been highly critical of President George W. Bush in his prosecution of the "War on Terror," but President Obama could not withstand the criticisms of Senator Obama. Beyond the moral inconsistencies of the policy approaches of the Obama Administration is the practical consequences of these drone killings. The bulging numbers of innocent civilians can only do harm to the interests of this nation. Do you think Americans are more terrorized than the people of Yemen, Afghanistan, or Pakistan? The Obama Administration claims of justified killings abroad are related to the claims of justified spying domestically.

National Security Agency Domestic Surveillance

The Fourth Amendment to the U.S. Constitution provides guarantees against the government engaging in conduct that would amount to unreasonable searches and seizures. Its express purpose is to curb the excesses of a powerful government, and to ensure that civil liberties are enjoyed by all who inhabit American society. The abuse of the tool of general warrants employed by the British crown was a driving force in the ratification of the article of the Bill of Rights. Sadly, the American government has not always complied by the supreme law of the land.

In the aftermath of the Watergate scandal, when in 1973 Congress found through investigation that the National Security Agency (NSA) had been spying on American citizens in violation of constitutional protections, a U.S. Senate Committee chaired by Frank Church (D., Idaho) made recommendations to prevent future abuses. Ultimately, in 1978 Congress passed the Foreign Intelligence Surveillance Act (FISA), that included the creation of a secretive tribunal known as the Foreign Intelligence Surveillance Court (FISC). This court handles matters related to domestic surveillance that is connected to interactions with foreign governments or nationals. The FISC operated largely in obscurity until the terrorist attacks of 11 September 2001. Within a matter of weeks Congress had rushed through legislation that was eagerly signed by then President George W. Bush. The USA PATRIOT Act is but one example of the consequence of fear dominated legislative efforts. The outcome of government responses to "9/11" has been the bloating of a national security apparatus that gobbles up resources and power, while trampling on constitutional protections. The balancing act between security and civil liberties has deteriorated into a dog and pony show of illegal activity reminiscent of government programs like COINTELPRO.

In a leaked NSA Inspector General Report dated 24 March 2009 it has been reported and confirmed that our government is deeply involved in a massive accumulation of data that is deeply private and personal. Despite his claims to the contrary, Senator Obama, and now President Obama has given his support to spying on Americans, without probable cause. As a senator he voted for amendments to FISA that have resulted in a danger-ously significant expansion of the government's claim of the legality of domestic surveillance. In fact, from 2009 to 2011 the NSA collected email and internet usage data of Americans under a program known as "Stellar Wind." This was done with FISC approval. In fact, our government is building a $2 billion data collection center known as the Utah Data Center that is scheduled to be "up and running" in September 2013. In fact, the "Stellar Wind" program launched during the first George W. Bush Administration was so secretive that only the Chief Judge of FISC was told of the program until 2006. There are eleven judges who sit on FISC. In fact, the FISA Amendments of 2008 granted retroactive legal immunity from liability to phone companies that cooperated in the illegal spying on Americans. In fact, then Attorney General Mukasey declared in 2008 that Internet Service Providers (ISPs) were also immune from liability.

Do not conclude that all Americans have simply accepted these over-reaches. Advocacy groups like the American Civil Liberties Union (ACLU), Amnesty International, the Center for Constitutional Rights (CCR), and the Electronic Frontier Foundation have pursued litigation strategies with predictably mixed results. As a student/reader you are encouraged to take a closer look at the following cases: *Al-Haramain Islamic Foundation v. Obama; Jewel v. NSA,* 673 F.3d 902 (Ct. App., 9th Cir., 2011); *Hepting v. AT&T; Clapper v. Amnesty International,* 568 U.S. _____ (2013); *CCR v. Obama;* and *Unitarian Church v. NSA.* The *Clapper* case is a U.S. Supreme Court case that challenged the 2008 FISA Amendments that authorized surveillance without a showing of probable cause. In a 5-4 decision, the Court held that Amnesty International lacked standing due to not being able to demonstrate a particular harm to particular individuals. Of course, that standing requirement is just about impossible to meet because the government will not reveal the specific targets of their domestic spying program. Moreover, the government has been successful in invoking the State Secrets Privilege in various courts. That evidentiary protection can be used as a shield merely based on the government's submitted affidavits. All that need be claimed is that the evidence (if revealed) might endanger national security. This circular legal logic is "Orwellian" in the most disturbing way.

Summarily, while the government proclaims secrecy to protect we Americans, many Americans wonder who will protect us from government secrecy. It is more than apparent that Congress will not. It is more than apparent that the courts will not. It is more than apparent that the President will not.

Notable Presidencies

A strong argument can be made that every presidency is a notable one because each one built the office into the tremendous standing it enjoys today. Many of the presidencies have been heightened or lessened only with the passing of time. What follows is a listing that is not all-inclusive, but that briefly discusses what is notable.

James Monroe: (1817–1825)

Monroe was noted for three major features, including the 1819 acquisition of Florida from Spain, the 1820 Missouri Compromise, and the 1823 Monroe Doctrine, which was crafted by his Secretary of State (and later President) John Quincy Adams. The Doctrine declared the Western Hemisphere to be under the exclusive jurisdiction of the United States, and set the stage for many interventions to follow in the Americas and the Caribbean. The Monroe administration is also known as the "Era of Good Feelings," where political partisanship greatly subsided.

Andrew Jackson: (1829–1837)

Jackson was noted for his steadfast destruction of Indians through the Seminole Wars, and the Indian Removal Act (cf. Trail of Tears). He was closely associated with the notion of territorial expansion and his support of slavery, and he was nicknamed "Old Hickory." Most importantly, he was the extremely partisan founder of the Democrat Party, and he gave that party the foundation of its southern, slavery base.

Abraham Lincoln: (1861–1865)

Lincoln was noted for his leadership during the Civil War. He was the first Republican president, and the first president to be assassinated. He is well-known for his Emancipation Proclamation that has been mislabeled as the instrument that freed the slaves, and for his Gettysburg Address.

Theodore Roosevelt: (1901–1909)

T. Roosevelt was noted for several things. He succeeded assassinated President William McKinley, and he was elected to office as a Republican in 1904. He later split the Republican Party in the 1912 election, running as the Bull Moose (Progressive) Party candidate. His splitting of the Republican votes between himself and incumbent William Howard Taft created enough of a rift to secure the Presidency for Democrat Woodrow Wilson. He remains as the youngest president to take office, and he was the first American to win a Nobel (Peace) Prize in 1906, even though he was an ardent warmonger. His "Square Deal" sought to fight for the betterment of the lives of the average American through regulating large corporations, and breaking up monopolies. He advocated universal health care one hundred years ago. In foreign matters he was a staunch interventionist, who added the Roosevelt Corollary to the Monroe Doctrine. That corollary is known as "walk softly, and carry a big stick." His image is joined by that of Washington, Jefferson, and Lincoln on Mount Rushmore.

Franklin Delano Roosevelt: (1933–1945)

F. D. Roosevelt was noted for his leadership through the domestic crisis of the Great Depression, and the foreign crisis of World War II. He was so wildly popular that he was elected to the presidency an unsurpassed four times. In fact, after his death the U.S. Constitution was changed to limit presidential terms. FDR's "New Deal" created an entire panoply of regulatory agencies and economic engines that created the modern welfare state. They included the Works Project Administration, the National Recovery Administration, the Social Security Administration, the Agricultural Adjustment Act, the Federal Deposit Insurance Corporation, the Tennessee Valley Authority, the National Labor Relations Board, the Securities and Exchange Commission, and the Civilian Conservation Corps. The continuing influence of the Roosevelt Administration is immeasurable. As the Commander-in-Chief of Armed Forces during World War II, FDR mobilized the military after the Pearl Harbor attack. He was single-handedly responsible for switching Black political allegiance from the Republican to the Democrat party. The industrial mobilization during WW II was the impetus for making the United States the world's greatest superpower, and for the ensuing decades of prosperity that were enjoyed by the middle class.

Lyndon Baines Johnson: (1963–1969)

Johnson was noted for his leadership on Civil Rights. He succeeded the assassinated, popular President John Fitzgerald Kennedy. LBJ went farther on Civil Rights as a southerner than the northern liberal JFK. His 1964 speech, "To Fulfill These Rights," is a must-read for any serious student of American politics. As a former Senate Majority Leader, he was a deft politician and legislator. Utilizing these skills, he pushed through Congress his "Great Society" legislative program that included his "War on Poverty." Unfortunately, not heeding the warnings of former President and Five-Star General Eisenhower about the rise of the military-industrial complex, his War on Poverty was lost in the fields of the War in Vietnam. His decision to escalate the War in Vietnam in the face of fierce Democrat Party opposition caused him not to seek reelection in 1968. His trail of successful legislation is quite deserving of mention. It included the Civil Rights Act (1964), the Food Stamp Act (1964), the Economic Opportunity Act (1964), the Higher Education Act (1965), the Social Security Act (1965), the Voting Rights Act (1965), the Immigration and Nationality Act (1965), the Freedom of Information Act (1966), the Fair Housing Act (1968), and the Gun Control Act (1968).

Richard Milhous Nixon: (1969–1974)

Nixon was noted for his corruption. The Nixon presidency is the only one to end in the resignation of the president. Nixon was the beneficiary of the massive social upheaval in America in the late 1960s. He was vice president in the 1950s in the Eisenhower Administration. He campaigned on a law-and-order domestic agenda, coupled with an end-the-Vietnam War foreign agenda. He accomplished neither goal. His criminal behavior calls into great question his claim of supporting law and order. In reality, he supported political repression. Instead of ending the war in Southeast Asia, he escalated it, including ordering the secret bombing of Cambodia, Laos, and North Vietnam. Nixon is the poster child for the excesses of the executive branch. As a sitting president, he pathetically tried to exert executive privilege to cover up his own felonious conduct. It took the U.S. Supreme Court in the case *United States v. Nixon* to have this president realize how far he had strayed from his solemn oath of office. When it was apparent that he would be impeached, and most likely successfully, his final cowardly act was to resign in disgrace, only to be pardoned by the very vice president he had appointed. This was the second vice president of his corrupt administration. Nixon's first vice president was Spiro T. Agnew. Agnew became only the second vice president in American history to resign his office, in 1973. John C. Calhoun had resigned more than a century earlier to take a U.S. Senate seat. But, Agnew resigned as part of a plea agreement to plead no contest to tax evasion and money-laundering charges stemming from his days as governor of Maryland.

Although criminality ran deep in his administration, Nixon did enjoy two foreign policy successes. He began the path to normalizing diplomatic relations with the People's Republic of China, and he was the architect of the policy of détente with the Soviet Union. The policy of détente slowed the nuclear arms race, and lessened tensions during the Cold War.

Ronald Wilson Reagan: (1981–1989)

Reagan was noted for several things. Reagan reinvigorated the American spirit after the humiliations suffered in the previous two administrations. Nixon was disgraceful, and Carter was impotent. It was during the Carter Administration that Americans were taken and held hostage by Iranian revolutionaries for 444 days. Even military attempts to free them were a dismal failure. With the nation humiliated and emasculated, Ronald Reagan provided an ego boost. Domestically, Reagan adopted economic policies that his own future Vice President called "voodoo economics" during the party nomination campaign. The notion that fiscal vitality can be maintained while cutting taxes on the wealthiest and spending one trillion dollars on defense is laughable. Even though the federal budget deficit exploded during the Reagan Administration, he was crafty enough to provide an essential ideological benefit. It was during the Reagan Administration that the Soviet Union collapsed under its own weight. In effect, the Reagan policies bankrupted the Soviet Union. Their disadvantage of not having a market-based economy caught up with them, and they were unable to continue spending on defense without seriously paralyzing basic services. The legacy left from the Reagan years is just beginning to wear under the weight of history. More and more Americans realize we cannot fail to regulate as Reagan proposed for many aspects of our economy. We also cannot make government the enemy of the people, as many who continue to espouse Reagan's conservative ideology are attempting to do. Nor can we pretend that tax cuts for the wealthiest among us will ensure a reinvestment in our economy that will benefit all. The trickle-down theory of the so-called Reagan Revolution has largely been discredited.

A quarter of a century later, we are sobering under the reality that the gap between rich and poor has exploded, and the middle class is the chump of supply-side economics. Consequently, if the lasting substance of the

Reagan Presidency domestically is exploding deficits, in foreign matters it is the ending of the Cold War.

As a matter of course, numerous presidents have sought to expand the power of the chief executive. It should now be apparent that this "dance" does not involve only the executive branch. Prior to and after the passage of the War Powers Act, Congress attempted to curb the excesses of several commanders-in-chief through legislative amendments. The first successful amendment passed through Congress and became law in 1973, just months before passage of the War Powers Act. It was called the Case-Church Amendment, and it purported to end direct U.S. military involvement in Southeast Asia. The most noteworthy of these congressional actions to limit the scope of presidential power was the Boland Amendment of 1984.

Iran-Contra Affair The Boland Amendment sought to prohibit the federal funding of Nicaraguan mercenaries, also known as the "Contras." The Reagan Administration was not willing to allow the Nicaraguan people to maintain their duly elected government. This was because of the leftist leanings of Nicaragua's revolutionary-minded Sandinista government. President Reagan was also quite sensitive to American hostages who were being held by the Iranian-based Hezbollah group. It was Reagan's willingness to violate the law in order to win freedom for the hostages that fueled the Iran-Contra Affair. The scheme was hatched by "rogue" members of the Reagan Administration. The initial idea was to sell arms to Iran through Israel in order to free the hostages. This was despite President Reagan's rather loud and untruthful proclamations that the United States does not negotiate with terrorists. This ill-conceived scheme eventually deteriorated into direct arms sales to Iran with a price markup that was diverted to fund the Contras in Nicaragua in direct violation of the Boland Amendment.

After high-profile Congressional hearings and indictments, not a single convicted criminal from the Reagan Administration spent any time in prison. Those whose convictions were not overturned for dubious technicalities were pardoned by President G.H.W. Bush. Several of these criminals served in the presidential administration of G. W. Bush.

The most important lesson from the Iran-Contra Affair was the exposure of a president's willingness to stoop to extralegal measures in order to carry out a foreign policy objective. The legacy of Ronald Reagan continues to be tarnished by his admission that he traded arms for hostages with a country the American government defined as terrorist. Also, Reagan's acknowledgment that a criminal enterprise was being directed from the basement of the White House by a Marine Corps Lieutenant Colonel (Oliver North) is quite damaging to his leadership rating.

Fall of Communism Regardless of your view of the Reagan years, there is one undeniable truth about his time as President. That truth is Reagan's personal facilitation of the fall of Communism. In the aftermath of the Reagan years, numerous former Eastern bloc countries declared their independence from Soviet Union hegemony and embraced some sort of free-market economic principles. Hence, while it is true that the major historical events associated with the fall of Communism occurred after the Reagan presidency, it is beyond question that Ronald Reagan was the architect of the collapse of the superpower then known as the Soviet Union. But revolutions like the mostly bloodless ones that swept Eastern Europe during the late 1980s and early 1990s do not come to fruition from external forces. Ronald Reagan needed a partner, and that partner was Soviet leader Mikhail Gorbachev. Gorbachev's policies of glasnost (openness) and perestroika (economic reform) were pivotal in the unraveling of Soviet reign. Again, the influence of military policies during the first term of the Reagan Administration was huge. In effect, what the United States was able to do was to use the Cold War nuclear arms race to financially bankrupt the Soviets. Particularly, the scientifically ridiculous Strategic Defense Initiative (SDI) motivated the Soviets to pour untold rubles into their already stretched military expenditures. One must be reminded that, at the same time, the Soviets were attempting to militarily conquer Afghanistan. That costly war with no end or victory depleted the Soviet economy, and, even more importantly, revealed a vulnerability that would have been unthinkable just a few years before. This is because, by all accounts, it was held that the strength of the Soviet military was its ground forces. The Soviet attempt to fight the Cold War and the war in Afghanistan proved too much. It is quite similar to attempts of the United States to fight the war in Iraq, the war in Afghanistan, and the War on Terror. Only time will tell whether our fate will be similar to that of the Soviets.

Nevertheless, the fall of the Soviet Union created an indictment against the basic tenets of Communism. Even China today has abandoned pronouncements of a Communist people's revolution, and has traded ideology for a market-based approach to their country's economic development. All of these changes are due to policies promoted by the Reagan Administration. It does not matter so much that the "Star Wars" defense system (SDI) was a crock from the outset. What matters is that the nuclear arms race was used to break the Soviet Union's economy, and the breakdown of their economy meant the breakdown of their empire in

Eastern Europe. It is quite predictable that much of the conservative ideology of the Reagan Administration will continue to tarnish, but the dividend of an emasculated Russia will likely withstand the test of time when thoughtful analyses of the impact of the Reagan Revolution begin to proliferate. Every president leaves some remembrance, whether big or small, and the fall of Communism is the one undisputable outcome of the presidency of Ronald Reagan.

As we examine historical developments as related to the Executive Branch, it will be evident that the table was set for Presidents G.H.W. Bush, Clinton, G. W. Bush, and Obama by their mentioned and unmentioned predecessors.

The musings of renowned sportswriter Grantland Rice in his poem, "Two Sides of War," illustrate the continuing problem of striking the proper balance between the power of Congress to declare and fund war, and the President's power to prosecute war.

G.H.W. Bush (1989–1993)

Following eight years of Ronald Reagan, there were four years of his loyal Vice President George H. W. Bush. Unlike Reagan, who had played heroes only in B movies, G.H.W. Bush was an authentic WWII hero. While he was a pilot, his plane was shot down over the Pacific, and he was plucked from the water. He was a former director of the Central Intelligence Agency. He had very close personal ties to the Saudi Royal Family. In fact, during the First Gulf War, he was able to convince the Saudi government to allow the amassing of a huge American military base on Saudi soil. This fact proved the impetus for the expansion of Al-Qaeda under the leadership of Osama bin-Laden. But, unlike his eldest son G. W. Bush, he was wise enough to assemble an array of allies to take on the raw military aggression of Saddam Hussein. This exemplifies a stark difference between the two wars in Iraq. The fact that the United States was leading a legitimate coalition of military forces against an aggressive tyrant gave legitimacy to the First Gulf War that has not been and will not be enjoyed by the current war in Iraq. Of course it must be revealed that Saddam Hussein was a monster of our making. At one time he was on the payroll of the very same CIA that G.H.W. Bush was leading. Moreover, even though the United States had claimed neutrality during most of the brutal war between Iraq and Iran in the 1980s, toward the end of that war we sided with Iraq, openly selling them military armaments. Openly is the operative word here because, as revealed in the Iran-Contra Affair, the United States sold armaments to both sides during the Iran-Iraq War. A reference to the classic Mary Shelley book, *Frankenstein,* is instructive here. As in the novel, the monster we created is the monster we eventually had to destroy.

But during the First Gulf War, President G.H.W. Bush made the decision to not destroy the monster of our creation, but to simply hobble him. In retrospect, that was most likely the wisest choice for both military and strategic reasons. Militarily, General Colin Powell impressed heavily upon the President that attempting to conquer Baghdad was not worth the great effort. Strategically, it was never in the best interest of the United States to create a vacuum of power in the already volatile and unstable so-called Middle East.

There are not many attributes of note to the G.H.W. Bush Administration. As an incumbent President, he was able to win his party's nomination, but he was not able to win the general election. He never enjoyed the enthusiastic support of the most powerful wing of his party because he was not a true conservative. He was a moderate whose conservative credentials were almost wholly dependent on his predecessor. Thus, he became a one-term president who is best remembered for saying: "read my lips; no new taxes," and then signing a bill that raised taxes. His thin legacy beyond the taxes debacle is that he trimmed a dictator we had created.

William Jefferson Clinton (1993–2001)

Few would argue with the tremendous personal charisma of Bill Clinton. His natural leadership skills and extraordinary intelligence have been his saving grace for his great personal flaw of philandering. Men do shape themselves after their most elevated hero, and in this case Bill Clinton mimicked approaches and behavior similar to those of John Fitzgerald Kennedy. When Clinton was just a teenager, he was honored by meeting President Kennedy at the White House. He went on from humble beginnings to graduate from Georgetown, attend Oxford as a Rhodes Scholar, and graduate from Yale Law School. At the tender age of thirty-two, he became the youngest governor in the nation's history. Like many other presidents, Bill Clinton went from being the chief executive of a state, to becoming the chief executive of a nation. In fact, more presidents have been former governors than any other elective office.

In all likelihood history will be kind to the Clinton years. There are several bases for this contention. First, the factual record is that Bill Clinton presided over the longest peacetime economic expansion in American history. Second, Bill Clinton reinvigorated the Democrat Party, much in the same way that Ronald Reagan had done for the Republican Party. Third,

Bill Clinton continues to enjoy immense popularity, even in the face of his many missteps as President, and even subsequent to his terms in office. His public approval ratings after his impeachment were higher than those of President Ronald Reagan when Reagan left office, also after two terms. Fourth, there is his mixed legislative record. And last, by utilizing a centrist approach, Bill Clinton left the template for political viability that can be instructive to either of the two major political parties.

Legislative Record With acknowledgment of the dangers of oversimplification, the Clinton Years were marked by domestic reforms and foreign failures. At the very least, President Clinton deserves some positive recognition for trying to address several intractable problems during his tenure in office. A glaring example of a courageous but failed attempt is his approach to health care reform in the early days of his first term. It is clear that if he had had another chance at his legislative agenda approach, he would have done things differently. Americans were unaccustomed to the assertiveness of a first lady like Hillary Rodham Clinton. Many bristled at her designation as the White House point person on health care reform. By all accounts, it was a miserable failure that still reverberates in the corridors of Capitol Hill. However, the silver lining of the ambitious attempt to provide better quality health care for more Americans was the signing of the Family and Medical Leave Act in 1993. This Act provided legal protection for employees who need to take care of loved ones. Although the Act has tended to be viewed as related to women taking time off for maternity care leave, it covers a much wider range of medical conditions.

Another area of legislative success was the 1993 signing of what is known as the Brady Bill. This gun control measure mandated a five-day waiting period on handgun purchases. Due to the power of anti-gun control forces, a portion of the law was ruled unconstitutional in the 1997 Supreme Court case *Printz v. United States.* The contention was that the Brady Bill was an unfunded mandate that impinged on states' Tenth Amendment rights under our system of federalism. In 1998, the waiting period provision expired, and it was rendered moot by the availability of the FBI's National Instant Criminal Background Check System (NICS).

A controversial domestic issue that was codified in federal law as signed by President Clinton is the Defense of Marriage Act (DOMA). This 1996 law defined marriage as a legal union exclusively between a man and a woman. The support this bill received in the House and Senate was overwhelming, but it raises extremely significant constitutional issues. There is a provision in DOMA that allows states to not recognize the legal force of same-sex marriages. According to the holding in the 1967 Supreme

Court case *Loving v. Virginia,* marriage is a fundamental right that states cannot abridge. According to the Due Process and Equal Protection Clauses of the Fourteenth Amendment to the U.S. Constitution, the sort of blatant discrimination in DOMA is not allowable. According to the Full Faith and Credit Clause of the U.S. Constitution, states are obligated to uphold the public records, proceedings, etc., of other states.

DOMA represents the paradox of Bill Clinton. The same President who earlier in his first term in office sought to give all gays and lesbians the right to serve openly in the United States Armed Forces signed a bill of dubious constitutionality like DOMA. There is no doubt that Bill Clinton felt the power of the blowback of his failed "Don't Ask; Don't Tell" compromise. That is the policy that was ultimately implemented as a fallback position to President Clinton's pathetic attempt to render sexual preference a nonfactor in who serves in our military. The policy has been a miserable failure.

Today this thorny issue is front and center in the culture war that undergirds the policy approaches of the two major parties.

Another area of legislative success for the Clinton Administration was welfare reform. In 1996, he signed the Personal Responsibility and Work Opportunity Act. This Act eliminated the Aid to Families with Dependent Children (AFDC) started by FDR in the height of the Great Depression. AFDC was replaced with Temporary Assistance for Needy Families (TANF), which ended welfare as an entitlement program. Entitlements are federal programs that guarantee benefits by law. Welfare reform under the Clinton Administration is also known as "workfare," because there was a two-consecutive-year limit placed on funds a recipient could collect before then being required to work. Also, TANF capped federal benefits in a lifetime to five years for any recipient. The result seemed to be positive for several years in terms of welfare caseloads, but the core problems of poverty and the working poor remain.

Yet another area of legislative success was in the signing of the North American Free Trade Agreement (NAFTA). This was the 1994 agreement between the U.S., Canada, and Mexico. Although it was a clear legislative victory for President Clinton, NAFTA is controversial in its effect on the U.S. economy. Some argue that NAFTA protects the interests of the ownership class in all three countries. Others argue that NAFTA has hurt workers in the United States by allowing manufacturing to be displaced to Mexico, and has hurt workers in Mexico by allowing cheap, subsidized agricultural products to flood their markets. Ironically, NAFTA enjoyed more support among Republicans than among members of President Clinton's own party.

The impact of the midterm election of 1994 on President Clinton's effectiveness cannot be overstated. When Congress opened for business in January 1995, it was the first time in 40 years that Republicans controlled the House of Representatives. That meant that the federal government was truly divided between a Democrat president, and Republican majorities in the Senate and House. Led by the later disgraced, but recently resurfaced Speaker of the House Newt Gingrich, Republicans published a Contract with America that outlined their conservative agenda. Soon thereafter, Senators Dole and McCain sponsored the Line Item Veto Act, which was signed into law by President Clinton in 1996. It is quite plausible that the desire of those two senators to occupy the White House was behind sponsoring an act that would have increased the power of the president. Nonetheless, the Line Item Veto Act can hardly be characterized as a legislative success because it was almost immediately challenged and declared unconstitutional in the 1998 Supreme Court case *Clinton v. City of New York.*

Domestic and Foreign Events Beyond a skeletal review of the Clinton Administration legislative record, there were several other domestic and foreign events that shaped the Clinton Years. First, there were the February 1993 bombing of the World Trade Center, the 1993 Branch Davidian massacre in Waco, Texas, the 1993 Battle of Mogadishu, the 1994 deployment of military forces to Haiti, the 1994 Rwandan genocide, the 1995 Federal Building bombing in Oklahoma City, the 1998 bombing of the U.S. Embassy in Nairobi, Kenya, the 2000 Elian Gonzales saga, and the 2000 attack on the *USS Cole* in the Gulf of Aden. Bill Clinton also made a last-ditch effort to resolve the Palestinian-Israeli conflict near the end of his second administration.

If we review it carefully, we see a pattern in the behavior of the Clinton Administration. There was a sort of dance between President Clinton and Congress. There was another sort of dance between passiveness and aggression in terms of foreign policy. There was certainly a willingness to try to make changes and shifts, but there was an overriding inconsistency with the resolve to follow through when opposition became stiff. For instance, during the Clinton Years, the United States suffered extremely damaging attacks domestically and abroad. It is obvious that the 1993 World Trade Center bombing should have been, but was not, enough to motivate the necessary level of vigilance. It is also obvious that the terrorists who bombed the Murrah Federal Building were doing so in response to the heavy-handed treatment and killings of eighty-two Branch Davidians in Waco, Texas. It is further obvious that the humiliation of American forces in Mogadishu created a reluctance to intervene in Africa that made Rwanda and Darfur worse than they should have been. These facts in turn created the vulnerabilities that were taken advantage of in the bombing of the U.S. Embassy in Nairobi, and in the attack on the *USS Cole* in the Gulf of Aden.

Overall, the Clinton Administration's handling of world events was a mixed bag of deftness, as in the case of normalizing relations with Vietnam, and incompetence, as in the case of protecting U.S. interests at home and abroad.

Clinton Impeachment Although history may be kind to whatever legacy is attributed to Bill Clinton, his personal conduct will always cast a shadow on his personal accomplishments. The skeletons that he dragged into the Oval Office eventually gained new life in the midst of the bitter partisanship that plagues "the Beltway." At the center of the media circus that became only the second presidential impeachment in American history was a man who could not restrain himself. Prior to becoming elected President, Bill Clinton had already amassed a trail of extramarital affairs. The allegations by a former Arkansas state employee named Paula Jones proved to be the impetus for a personal embarrassment that was difficult to witness. By the time that Ms. Jones and her attorneys were paid approximately $850,000 to settle her case against her former boss, several lives and careers had been wrecked. To this day it is perplexing to consider why a man of such extraordinary intellect could behave like such a buffoon.

The U.S. Constitution provides for the removal of a sitting president through the process known as impeachment. This is an important component of the concept of checks and balances. However, the Constitution dictates that impeachment is only proper for high crimes and misdemeanors. There is still a debate about whether the conduct of President Clinton constituted high crimes and misdemeanors. He was impeached by a lame duck Congress in December 1998. There were two charges, perjury and obstruction of justice. The perjury charge involved President Clinton's deposition in the Paula Jones matter. He was accused of lying under oath about whether he had had sexual relations with a White House intern by the name of Monica Lewinsky. The obstruction of justice charge was based on his efforts to cover up his marital infidelity with young Ms. Lewinsky. As strange as it may seem, the facts of the impeachment are not nearly as important as the politics that drove the impeachment proceedings. Even though in 1996 and 1998 Democrats regained seats lost in the 1994 election, Republican control over the House and Senate is what drove our nation to the folly of the Clinton impeachment. It is abundantly clear through subsequent events that many citizens did not desire nor enjoy the attempt to destroy a twice-elected, popular president for his woeful personal conduct. Of the thirteen Republican House "managers" who prosecuted the impeachment trial, only three are still members of Congress. Moreover, for all its pronouncements on family values, several prominent Republicans have been exposed as frauds through their own personal scandals.

When all was said and done, the impeachment attempt failed miserably. To convict on either charge, there needed to be at least sixty-seven senators voting that way. Of the fifty-five conviction votes on the perjury charge, not a single one was from a Democrat. Only fifty senators voted to convict on the obstruction of justice charge, again without a single Democrat vote. In the aftermath, Washington was a more divided, more dysfunctional, meaner place. More importantly, the consequences of impeachment as a charade have been to reduce any toleration for another impeachment in the foreseeable future. This is significant, because a much more plausible argument was available to impeach members of the G. W. Bush Administration for potential high crimes and misdemeanors such as the dishonesty leading up to the Iraq invasion of 2003, and the behavior of convicted criminals such as Vice President Cheney's former Chief of Staff Scooter Libby. Whatever one may think of the personal conduct of Bill Clinton, he cannot be held responsible for the deaths of thousands of American military personnel, and hundreds of thousands of Iraqi and Afghani citizens as can our forty-third Commander-in-Chief. The resultant effect was to greatly increase the cynicism of the American public, and to greatly decrease the confidence in our political leaders' ability to solve our nation's problems.

W (2001–2009)

If there is a likelihood that history will be kind to Bill Clinton, the opposite can be stated about the years in the Oval Office for George Walker Bush. The fallout of his eight years in our highest office continues to have an impact like that of ocean air corrosion. Like his predecessor, W was able to make a successful White House run after enjoying an effective stint as the governor of a state. Not to be confused with flattery, there is something unique about politicians from Texas. The legacy of the G. W. Bush years could very well have as significant an effect for the Republican Party as the influence of Ronald Reagan. But, the telling difference is that

Reagan strengthened his party, whereas W greatly weakened the Republican Party's prominence in national politics. This is because, even though Reagan espoused conservative tenets, he was also appealing to nonconservatives. In the case of G. W. Bush, he espoused conservative tenets that he did not follow, and his appeal narrowed to the point where other Republicans disassociated themselves from him. Bush narrowed the appeal of the Republican Party at a time when the American electorate was becoming broader, less white, and less conservative. He single-handedly trashed the notion that Republicans are fiscally responsible by more than doubling the national debt. He attempted to use personal character as a draw, but greatly deceived the nation in trying to make a cogent case to go to war against a country that had done nothing to Americans. The bungling ineptitude of others in his administration seemed to result in accolades and promotions. His fierce Texan brand of loyalty seemed to eclipse the importance of the task at hand. When then Secretary of State Colin Powell expressed discomfort with the prosecution of the War in Iraq, he was replaced by Condoleeza Rice. This would not have been so bad if it weren't for the fact that she failed as National Security Advisor to protect the nation against the 9/11 terrorists. Many Americans will not forget the image of Dr. Rice being questioned before Congress about a memo that boldly predicted that Osama bin Laden would attack the World Trade Center using jet airplanes. Bush's decision-making skills, or lack thereof, cost the nation more than it cost him. As a conservative he breathed life into the corpse of the trickle-down-theory, and he obstructed nearly every attempt at Congressional oversight. His deregulatory posture ultimately made possible and probable the economic meltdown that occurred in his second term. In the last year of his presidency, 2.6 million American jobs were lost, and this free-market conservative had to swallow hard while taxpayer money was used to bail out financial institutions that had greedily careened the economy toward systemic risk. Unfortunately, none of this is surprising to those who have studied America's political history. It is no stretch that a man who literally cheated his way into office would have such a low regard for government service, and the rule of law.

November 2000 Election There have been at least three other presidential elections where the person who achieved the largest number of popular votes did not become president. It happened in 1800, 1824, 1876, and 2000. The fact is that Vice President Al Gore won the popular vote, and he won the Electoral College vote. After the Florida debacle, several newspapers used the Freedom of Information Act to gain access to the ballots in Florida. Had it not been for the judicial activism of conservative members of the U.S. Supreme Court, the Florida recount as ordered by the State Supreme Court would have revealed that Al Gore won the popular vote in Florida, and should have received Florida's twenty-five Electoral College votes and become the forty-third President of the United States. The disfranchisement of thousands of Floridians through numerous forms of official malfeasance needs to be entered into the annals of American political disgrace. The Secretary of State of Florida, who is responsible for ensuring fair elections, was simultaneously the Co-Chair of the Bush Election campaign in the state. The official margin of victory of 537 votes of over 6 million cast was smaller than the number of Black men who were not allowed to vote because their names had been removed from registration rolls. The problem is that the felon purge list that was the brainchild of the Office of the Secretary of State had such loose parameters that Black men without any criminal record were not allowed to cast their vote. Of the Black Floridians who did cast a ballot, over 85% voted for Vice President Al Gore. Entire Florida counties that had historically voted for the Democrat candidate were showing returns favoring conservative Republican Patrick Buchanan. The irregularities go on, and were well documented in the United States Commission on Civil Rights Report that was compiled in the aftermath of the November 2000 election.

Bush v. Gore In a civil society, disputes are handled by the supposed neutral arbiters of the judiciary. Many legal scholars were shocked that the U.S. Supreme Court granted certiorari in the election dispute. For years the Rehnquist Court had trumpeted states' rights. Now, with the credibility of the Republic at issue, the Court by a five-to-four margin stopped the recount in Florida, which in effect handed the election to G. W. Bush. This was the finest hour for judicial activism. The case will live in infamy, and a harbinger is the fact that the opinion stated that the case could not be used as legal precedent. One can easily understand why the holding was limited to the case at hand. The twisted legal logic applied was so onerous, particularly since the method of disfranchisement used in Florida was the very sort of racism that the Equal Protection Clause of the Fourteenth Amendment sought to end. Yet, the Republican appointees on the Court claimed that G. W. Bush's rights were being violated under the Clause because the Florida Supreme Court-ordered statewide recount would be performed differently in Florida's different counties. The dissent of Justice John Paul Stevens speaks volumes:

"What must underlie petitioners' entire federal assault on the Florida election procedures is an unstated lack of confidence in the impartiality and capacity of the state judges who would make the critical decisions if the vote count were to proceed. Otherwise, their position is wholly without merit. The endorsement of that position by the majority of this Court can only lend credence to the most cynical appraisal of the work of judges throughout the land. It is confidence in the men and women who administer the judicial system that is the true backbone of the rule of law. Time will one day heal the wound to that confidence that will be inflicted by today's decision. One thing, however, is certain. Although we may never know with complete certainty the identity of the winner of this year's Presidential election, the identity of the loser is perfectly clear. It is the Nation's confidence in the judge as an impartial guardian of the rule of law."

Again, is it reasonable to think that a man who was not the choice of the majority of the American electorate would lead in a respectable way? The folly that followed can only merit so much shock value. The spectacle of the presidential motorcade to G. W. Bush's first inauguration being pelted with eggs did not make the network news, but the sense of a fundamental miscarriage of justice still stings for some.

Legislative Record G. W. Bush's legislative record is less than impressive for the main reason of his good fortune of having his party in control of both chambers of Congress for much of his tenure in office. Because there was not a divided government until 2007, President Bush used the veto power less than any president in recent memory. Of his twelve vetoes, four were overridden. The first (Stem Cell Research Enhancement Act of 2005) was not until July 2006. His legislative victories included the USA PATRIOT Act of 2001, the No Child Left Behind Act of 2002, and the Medicare Prescription Drug, Improvement, and Modernization Act of 2003. Each of these three laws has its critics. The USA PATRIOT Act has been criticized as an unconstitutional attack on civil liberties. The No Child Left Behind Act has been criticized as an unfunded mandate that places too much emphasis on standardized test results as an indication of academic improvement. The Medicare Act has been criticized as more than four times as expensive as it was represented to members of Congress.

There were also huge failures in Bush's legislative agenda. Two that stand out are Social Security reform, and immigration reform. President Bush's plan to privatize Social Security was met with a great deal of skepticism. The usual Republican attempts to characterize government as the enemy was not effective in convincing the growing legions of baby boomers that their retirement would be handled best through the roller coaster of investment markets. Immigration reform predictably failed due to sensitivities to issues such as amnesty, and the white xenophobia concerning the browning of America. Although the Republican Party could afford not to act on Social Security, the failure to implement immigration reform truly damaged the objective of diversifying the allegiance to the party. The racism of conservative policies was stripped of its thin veneer, and the courtship between Latinos and the Republican Party fizzled.

As the Bush legislative agenda floundered, President Bush resorted to abusing a tool at the disposal of presidents for many decades. When President Bush found himself in the position of not being politically able or willing to veto legislation, he leaned heavily on the use of presidential signing statements. Only seventy-five such signing statements were issued from Presidents Monroe through Reagan. But, beginning with President Reagan, their use has exploded. President G. W. Bush issued presidential signing statements that disturbingly objected to provisions in the law he had just signed in close to four out of five cases. What began as a ceremonial gesture has turned into a tool that undermines the rule of law and the separation of powers.

War on Terror   In many ways the G. W. Bush years were like the George Orwell novel *1984*. The blind trust placed in a president during times of crisis is reminiscent of General George Patton's statement, "If everyone is thinking alike, then somebody isn't thinking." After the September 11, 2001, attacks on the World Trade Center and the Pentagon, Americans once again allowed fear to trump values. Because the fear was not reasonable, phobia would be a more apt description. In slightly more than thirty days, the U.S. Congress had given the Bush Administration a virtual blank check to wage an ethereal war against an ethereal enemy. What followed was a repetition in futility not unlike the fight against the concept of a "Red Scare." The new McCarthyism was just as arrogant as the old. President Bush in public pronouncements said things like "Axis of Evil," equated Saddam Hussein with Adolf Hitler, and declared that you were either with us, or against us. For a country such as America that was founded on dissent and rebellion, this browbeating of agreement as an equation to patriotism was farcical. Never mind that most of the 9/11 perpetrators were Saudi nationals, and that none was Iraqi. When no Americans could fly in the hours after the attacks, over twenty members of the Saudi Royal Family were allowed to fly out of the country. People who were mistaken for Muslims were attacked, and they were sometimes murdered in this country.

Accordingly our methods and policies changed, but not in concert with our stated values. We were told they knew better, and they were doing the ugly things to protect us. We began spying on our own citizenry without warrants in violation of the Fourth Amendment to the Constitution. We began kidnapping (for lack of a better term) suspects throughout the globe and sending them to places where they could be "convinced" to share information with our intelligence operatives. We called it rendition. We hired mercenaries with the titles of private contractors, such as Blackwater, to kill in our name. We are still trying to figure out what authority applies to them and their conduct. We held members of our military beyond their commitments and gave them substandard equipment. In classic Orwellian doublespeak we have allowed the Bush Administration to refer to torture as "enhanced interrogation techniques." We have opened a high-security military detention facility on the soil of a sovereign nation where we have no right to be. At Camp X-Ray at Guantanamo Bay, Cuba, the current president is trying to unravel the mess made by Bush's War on Terror. Can we maintain our credibility as a nation under the rule of law if we indefinitely hold prisoners without even charging them? Are the U.S. Supreme Court repudiations of the Bush approach in the 2004 cases *Rasul v. Bush* and *Hamdi v. Rumsfeld,* the 2006 case *Hamdan v. Rumsfeld,* and the 2008 case *Boumediene v. Bush* sufficient to restore the credibility of our established jurisprudence?

In the *Rasul* case the Court determined that it had jurisdiction to hear cases involving foreign nationals held at Guantanamo Bay. In the *Hamdi* case, the Court determined that U.S. citizens detained as unlawful enemy combatants have the right to access to the civilian judicial system through habeas corpus petitions. In the *Hamdan* case, the Court determined that President Bush did not have the authority to have habeas corpus petitions heard before military tribunals, even in light of Congress passing the Detainee Treatment Act of 2005. In the *Boumediene* case, the Court determined that the Military Commissions Act of 2006 violated the detainee's right to have his habeas corpus petition heard in civilian courts in the U.S. After years of legal wrangling, one thing is crystal clear: even a Supreme Court with a conservative majority finds no legal basis for the Bush approach to the War on Terror. Two acts of Congress have been swept aside as inadequate to protect the rights of suspected terrorists.

Today, the Obama Administration is struggling with what to do with this special class of detainees. However, the world is watching and waiting for a more respectable approach to those who are (in some cases) not even charged with a crime. The tradition of habeas corpus goes back almost 800 years. The Bush approach of treating detainees as if they were convicts flies in the face of all that we claim that we stand for. If they are guilty, let us put it to a fair trial, not a dog-and-pony show of military tribunals with inadequate legal protections, and predictable outcomes.

Hurricane Katrina It is always fascinating to observe whether there is any change or improvement in a second-term President's leadership skills. In the case of President G. W. Bush, Hurricane Katrina was an opportunity to show that he had learned something from his rough first term. Instead we are left with the image of the President looking out a window of Air Force One, high above the suffering of his people. But, were they his people? Had he done anything to relieve the suffering of darker-hued and more-impoverished Americans? It was a poetic and iconic revelation similar to Nero fiddling while Rome burned. By the time President Bush touched down on the ground in New Orleans, everything had the vacuous air of a photo shoot. He had the temerity to appear with and congratulate Michael Brown, the incompetent Director of the Federal Emergency Management Agency (FEMA). Brown had been elevated to his position by a crony of the President, even though he had no previous experience in managing emergencies. On 2 September 2005, President Bush exclaimed on national television: "Brownie, you're doing a heck of a job." That night at a fundraiser, entertainer Kanye West spoke truth to power by criticizing the media coverage of events on the ground in New Orleans by saying: "You see a black family, it says, They're looting. You see a white family, it says, They're looking for food. George Bush doesn't care about black people." Ten days later, the man praised by the President had his resignation accepted by the President. In 2006 testimony before Congress, Brown virtually stated that he was the fall guy, and said that President Bush's ignoring his warnings about the levees and the preoccupation with counterterrorism by the Department of Homeland Security were to blame for the lapse in leadership and governmental response to Hurricane Katrina.

Leadership is an intangible that Americans expect and demand from the President. Hurricane Katrina was bad for race relations, Bush's integrity, and the Republican Party. There was a widespread impression that because the faces of suffering were Black and poor there was little priority given to help. This appalled the vast majority of Americans and offended their sensibilities. It also reminded the nation that we had lost the priority of taking care of our own. When the tsunami hit Indonesia in December 2004, the U.S. government placed relief supplies on the ground half-way around the world within hours. When the hurricane hit the Gulf Coast, the U.S. government took weeks to provide basic supplies such as water, food, and shelter. The magnitude of the disaster was precisely what our National Guard was formulated to respond to. But so many resources were devoted to Iraq that Black and impoverished citizens were left to devolve into grotesque caricatures of humans under the weight of despair. The crisis in response revealed a crisis in leadership that cut directly to policy decisions of where and how our federal resources would be allocated. The President is the leader of her or his party and the nation. When the leadership of the nation is poor, the leadership of the party is poor. Hurricane Katrina cemented the domestic legacy of George W. Bush as one that Americans knew was deeply violative of the spirit of our national motto, *E Pluribus Unum*. The ramifications of Katrina extended the perception of President Bush as inert, and a lame duck with over three full years left in his final term.

2006 Midterm Election The 2006 midterm election trouncing of the Republicans was a direct consequence of an American political landscape littered with failed Bush initiatives. Again, the message fell on deaf ears. Unwilling to recognize the midterm election as a referendum on his War in Iraq, Bush increased the U.S. troop presence instead of ramping down the occupation. Along with other events mentioned, and yet to be detailed, President Bush set the table for the demise of his Party's influence. His approval rating in the waning days of his Presidency would never reach any more than a third of the polled respondents.

Obama (2009–Present)

Political scientists will be revising their texts about presidential campaigns for some time to come due to the phenomenal success of Barack Hussein Obama II. Never before had a candidate been able to raise such astounding amounts of money. For the first time since the enactment of campaign financing laws in 1976, a major party candidate refused public financing in a general election. This is understandable, considering that the campaign raised over $670 million. However, what is most impressive about Barack Obama's campaign donations is that the average amount given was less than $200.00.

Besides financing, there was a tremendous amount of political savvy displayed in order for an African American with a compelling personal story, but with thin political credentials, to defeat the machine candidate. Few gave the junior senator from Illinois a chance to defeat the junior senator from New York. After all, Hillary Clinton enjoyed deep ties to the White House as a former First Lady. She appeared to be unbeatable, with her war chest of funds, and long list of important backers. It was no secret that whoever won the Democrat Party nomination had the inside line to becoming the next resident of 1600 Pennsylvania Avenue. There was also an intrigue to getting a "two-for-one" deal in terms of Senator Clinton, and former President Clinton. Additionally, it seemed a logical and well-orchestrated rise, not only for Senator Clinton, but for women in general.

However, Senator Clinton's political strategists horribly miscalculated the hunger for change in 2008. Largely because of her refusal to acknowledge her mistake in supporting the Iraq War, Senator Clinton began to look like business as usual in a time of change. She coupled that blunder with the even larger error of expecting no serious opponents beyond Super Tuesday. As it turned out, the sense of her invulnerability was shattered when Barack Obama won the Iowa Caucus. If this Black man could win in a state as white as Iowa, perhaps he could win in November. Once he became a serious consideration for winning the general election, she was in deep trouble. Her decision not to contest other caucuses, and to concentrate only on big state primaries was her candidacy's death knell. Consequently, her fundraising capacities began to dry up at the very time when Senator Obama was using the Internet to scoop money up like manna from heaven.

Then, Bill Clinton began to appear to be more of a liability than an asset. His disrespectful comments about the Obama mania sweeping the nation as the campaign trail swung into the South had tinges of racism. The perception that the Clintons were playing the race card was greatly damaging. This was beyond foolish, taking into account that Blacks had been greatly loyal to the Clintons, especially to the former president. All of a sudden there seemed to be this strange imbalance of it being completely acceptable for women to vote for Senator Clinton because she was a woman, but completely unacceptable for African Americans to vote for Senator Obama because he was Black. Of course these are oversimplifications, but in political campaigns perceptions frequently trump realities.

By November, Barack Obama had realized the very meaning of his name (blessed). With the oratory skills befitting an African man from a people of strong oral history traditions, a coolness that was also hip, and a hipness that was also cool, President Obama strolled into world history. He did receive great assistance from the unpopularity of nearly all Republicans, extraordinary charisma engulfed in strong family values, and an opponent in Senator McCain who was well past his time, and his prime. One must also give an assist to the former point guard and Governor of the State of Alaska, who was a cynical pick at best. Clearly unqualified to be President, she paled in comparison to Senator Joseph Biden, the same way McCain did with Obama. Hence, Obama's choice of running mate was equally as good as McCain's was bad. On election night, Obama won 53% of the vote and 365 Electoral College votes, and McCain won 46% of the vote and 173 Electoral College votes. More importantly, America entered a new phase of leadership that symbolically destroyed any limitation or artificial barrier concerning our future as an inclusive society.

Be Careful of What You Ask For As riveting as the 2008 general election was, it was merely a trailer to the feature film. In January 2009, President Obama took power and took control of the biggest economic mess since the Great Depression. Some of his first official acts were to issue executive orders to the military to develop plans to end the War in Iraq, and to close the naval station at Guantanamo Bay. These have proved thorny enough problems to cause the President to adjust his campaign promises, but he seems on the pathway to try to live up to what the majority of the American people want him to do.

Legislatively, his first bill signed was the Lilly Ledbetter Fair Pay Act of 2009, which has the effect of overturning the Supreme Court's 2007 decision in the employment discrimination case, *Ledbetter v. Goodyear Tire and Rubber Company.* Just days later, he signed the Children's Health Insurance Reauthorization Act of 2009. This Act provides states with matching funds to cover millions of children who would otherwise not be eligible for health insurance. Known by the acronym SCHIP, it was the outcome of the failed health care reform of the Clinton Administration. In December 2007, President G. W. Bush vetoed similar proposed legislation.

In these first months of the Obama Administration, the most significant piece of new legislation is the American Recovery and Reinvestment Act of 2009. Commonly known as the economic stimulus package, it provides $787 billion in spending, and has placed the broadest symbolic grin on the otherwise stoic countenance of the late John Maynard Keynes. It is far too early to give a credible assessment on the effectiveness of this law, but charges of socialism and government takeovers of private industry are far overblown.

Change There has been a great deal made by the President of wanting to change the way Washington works. The greatest test of his desire of a less partisan relationship among the three branches will be President Obama's insistence on health care reform by the end of 2009. In many regards, he has already changed the Beltway just by virtue of his presence. It is quite astounding that a Black man is leading a government that has never lived up to its obligations to Black people. It is also remarkable that the

President seems to be a great manager of the multiple serious crises facing our nation and our world. The world is eager to see a more credible, robust, and progressive United States of America.

President Obama has nominated a Latina to sit on the highest court for the first time. The list of "firsts" will continue to grow, but, in what form is the operative inquiry. Given his record of personal accomplishments, it is risky to doubt his ability to do what is important to him. But, he definitely has a host of detractors. Some are legitimate, and some have a political ax to grind. As a matter of personality, President Obama seeks the middle ground, and he does not appear to fully grasp that those who do not share his view want nothing to do with resolutions, because resolutions increase his status. President Obama has a majority of members of his own party in the House and the Senate. In fact, with the legal determination that Al Franken won the Senate race in Minnesota, and the news that he will sit on the Judiciary Committee, the President looked to have a supermajority in the Senate. But it was not to be. It would have been fascinating to see if he could package one-party rule as some semblance of bipartisanship. The Republicans have no real interest in supporting his legislative agenda, nor most of his policies. There are two checks on his undeniable power, though. The most troublesome is his own party members. The other is the conservative majority on the Supreme Court, but that could change. The potential for Judge Sotomayor to replace retiring Justice Souter doesn't indicate any real shift. Nor has the additional of another woman, Elena Kagan. But, if Justice Thomas, Justice Scalia, or Justice Kennedy should leave the Bench during an Obama Administration, there would be a major upheaval in the legal universe.

Americans want the type of leadership that President Obama seemed able to provide. But the "bloom is off the rose" now. A man who appeared to be deferential to the rule of law, and a former Constitutional Law Professor with a stellar academic pedigree, he embodies the American Dream. However, misstep after misstep has only heightened skepticism toward our government, and its leaders. His unquestionable charm, youthful vigor, and resoluteness are refreshing to many, but not enough for most. Unlike his Republican counterparts, he seemed to be beyond the ugly reach of personal scandal, mean-spiritedness, and hypocrisy. But, from which position on the political spectrum shall he govern? In his first administration, he never could find the most effective alchemy. He is not the traditional liberal the media like to paint him as, but he is also neither centrist nor conservative. One thing is for sure, of all the Chief Executives he is unique.

Chapter 5
Study Guide

1. Which of the following states does not use the winner-take-all system in presidential elections?

   a: Hawaii   d: Maine
   b: Missouri   e: Oregon
   c: Puerto Rico

2. Which President appointed the most women to his Cabinet?

   a   George W. Bush   d: George H. W. Bush
   b: Bill Clinton   e: Barack Obama
   c: Richard Nixon

3. Approximately how much money did Presidential candidate Barack Obama raise in his (2008) quest for the White House?

   a: $700 thousand   d: $70 billion
   b: $700 million   e: $70 million
   c: $700 billion

4. Which of the following *is not* one of the 3 constitutional qualifications for the office of president?

   a: natural born citizen
   b: be a white man
   c: 35 years of age
   d: be a 14-year resident of the U.S.

5. The group that now controls the nomination process for president is the:

   a: mass public
   b: party elites
   c: mass media
   d: presidential nominees themselves

6. The framers of the Constitution established the Electoral College because they wanted:
   a: to ensure the general population would have an opportunity to directly vote for the president
   b: the choice of president and vice-president to be made by a few dispassionate, reasonable men
   c: only candidates for president and vice-president who graduated from the Electoral College
   d: the political parties to be able to control the selection of president and vice-president

7. The major parties are not in favor of eliminating the Electoral College because:
   a: the founding fathers wanted it that way
   b: our system is the best in the world
   c: constitutional amendments are tough to pass
   d: they fear it would give minor parties a more influential role in elections

8. How can the President check/balance Congress?
   a: she/he can not
   b: through use of the veto power
   c: through public opinion
   d: through news conferences

9. The term "human bomb" refers to:
   a: changing the facts on the ground
   b: biological warfare
   c: infant mortality rates
   d: none of the choices

10. This massive economic rebuilding effort was put into action after World War II:
    a: the Keynesian Plan
    b: the Marshall Plan
    c: Perestroika
    d: Glasnost
    e: containment

11. The most common occupation of presidents has been:
    a: politicians
    b: governors
    c: capitalists
    d: lawyers

12. In the event that no candidate receives a majority of the Electoral College votes, the president is selected:

    a: by the Senate   c: by the People

    b: by the House   d: by the Supreme Court

13. Can the president remove federal judges from office?

    a: yes   c: sometimes

    b: maybe   d: no

14. The role in which the president has probably exercised more authority than in any other role is _____.

    a: party leader   c: moral leader

    b: Commander-in-Chief   d: media mogul

15. What is the only requirement of a president in issuing an executive order?

    a: that it be written

    b: that it be verbal

    c: that it be true

    d: that it be published in the Federal Register

16. The ability of the president to withhold certain information from Congress and/or the courts is based on:

    a: pure power   c: congressional privilege

    b: abuse of power   d: executive privilege

17. Which constitutional amendment established procedures for presidential succession and disability?

    a: 25th   c: 29th

    b: 27th   d: 12th

18. Which Congressional Act resolved the question of who shall be president if both the president and vice president die?

    a: The Presidential Act of 2004   c: The Succession Act of 1947

    b: The National Act of 1941   d: The Act of the Apostle

19. Which government official is third in line of succession to the presidency?

    a: vice president   c: Secretary of State

    b: governor   d: Senate president pro tempore

20. Who were the two presidents impeached by the House of Representatives?

    a: Nixon and Clinton   c: Johnson and Clinton

    b: Nixon and Johnson   d: Nixon and Bush

21. The foreign policy that allows the U.S. to sell weapons to dictators who support American business interests around the world and to repel terrorism with force is the policy of:

    a: détente   c: counterintelligence

    b: moral idealism   d: political realism

22. One major reason for the massive increase in U.S. public debt in recent years is:

    a: massive increases in social welfare spending

    b: the wars in Iraq and Afghanistan

    c: new prison construction

    d: tax increases on the rich

23. Concern over nuclear weapon proliferation intensified in 1999 when the Senate rejected the:

    a: China/North Korea Treaty

    b: Comprehensive Nuclear Test Ban Treaty

    c: Middle East Peace Treaty

    d: Nuclear Terrorism Treaty

24. The Powell Doctrine states each of the following about the U.S. entering war except:

    a: there should be a clear, obtainable objective

    b: we should strike our enemies before they strike us

    c: all other nonviolent means have been exhausted

    d: the action should be supported by the American people

    e: there should be genuine, broad international support

25. The major provision of the War Powers Act was to:

    a: limit the president's use of troops in military action without congressional approval

    b: allow the president more freedom in the use of military troops throughout the world

    c: give the president new powers in the area of foreign policy

    d: prevent aggressor nations from becoming too strong militarily

26. The event that signified the Soviet Union had relinquished its political and military control over the states of Eastern Europe was the:

    a: renewed interest in Cuba
    b: fall of the Berlin Wall
    c: defeat in Afghanistan
    d: dissolution of the Soviet Union

27. The United States ran a budget surplus under the presidency of:

    a: Ronald Reagan   c: Bill Clinton
    b: Jimmy Carter   d: George W. Bush

28. The Monroe Doctrine states that the U.S.:

    a: had territorial dominion over South America
    b: was neutral in its relations with Europe and Asia
    c: could trade openly with China
    d: would not accept foreign intervention in the Western Hemisphere

29. Foreign policy based on moral imperatives is often unsuccessful for the U.S. because it:

    a: makes policy making difficult to understand
    b: assumes that other nations agree with American views of morality and politics
    c: requires the president to establish absolute standards of conduct for U.S. personnel
    d: makes too many enemies

30. What was the official margin of victory for Bush in FL (2000)?

    a: 735   d: 1776
    b: 175,000   e: 537
    c: 1784

31. How many votes were never included in the Florida 2000 presidential election count?

    a: none   d: 383
    b: all of them   e: 537
    c: 175,000

32. What mechanism was used in the Florida 2000 presidential election to disenfranchise Black voters?

   a: bait and switch
   b: affirmative action
   c: hanging chads
   d: felon purge list
   e: Katherine Harris

33. How many illegal absentee ballots were in the final tally certified by FL Sec. of State Katherine Harris?

   a: 68,800
   b: 8660
   c: 68
   d: 6880
   e: 680

34. How many blank conviction dates were there on FL's felon purge list?

   a: 4,000
   b: 400,000
   c: 4 million
   d: 40,000
   e: 40 million

35. How many votes were never certified in FL 2000?

   a: 750
   b: 750,000
   c: 666
   d: 75,000
   e: 175,000

36. In the Florida 2000 presidential election, how many so-called "ex offenders" were purged from the voting lists?

   a: 383
   b: none
   c: 175,000
   d: 2883
   e: 75,000

37. Which "third party" may have cost Democrat Al Gore the presidency in the 2000 election?

   a: Peace and Freedom
   b: Libertarian
   c: Natural Rights
   d: Green

38. Which of the following *was not* an issue of irregularity in the Ohio 2004 presidential election vote?

   a: felon purge list
   b: electronic voting machines
   c: voter registration
   d: voter suppression

39. According to exit polls conducted after the Ohio 2004 presidential election, _____ was winning by millions of votes:

    a: Nader
    b: Bush
    c: Gore
    d: Guiliani
    e: Kerry

40. Which of these tools did G.W. Bush frequently use to subvert the Madisonian Model?

    a: the pocket veto
    b: the war on Iraq
    c: the bully pulpit
    d: recess appointments
    e: presidential signing statements

41. According to the Congressional Research Service approximately how many times did G.W. Bush challenge laws through signing statements, and on what theory/doctrine?

    a: 100/conspiracy theory
    b: 160/unitary executive theory
    c: 500/imperial doctrine
    d: 140/big bang theory
    e: he never has

42. G.W. Bush's foreign policy of "getting them before they get us" is known as:

    a: cowboy up
    b: preemptive action
    c: sabre rattling
    d: gunboat diplomacy

43. Which "liberal" president ordered Japanese Americans into concentration camps during WWII?

    a: Ronald Reagan
    b: Woodrow Wilson
    c: FDR
    d: LBJ
    e: BLT

44. The president who warned the nation of the influence of the military-industrial complex was:

    a: Eisenhower
    b: Nixon
    c: Reagan
    d: Clinton

45. From the 1820s to the 1980s, about how many times were presidential signing statements used?

    a: 750
    b: 75
    c: 350
    d: 35
    e: 500

46. Identify the two U.S. presidents who had the lowest and highest percentages (respectively) of objecting to provisions within laws they signed [through signing statements]:

a: Clinton/G.W. Bush
b: Clinton/Reagan
c: G.H.W. Bush/G.W. Bush
d: Reagan/G.H.W. Bush

47. Who received the most infamous presidential pardon?

a: Scooter Libby
b: Richard Nixon
c: G. Gordon Liddy
d: Charles Lindbergh
e: Dick Cheney

48. Is a line item veto constitutional?

a: yes
b: no
c: maybe
d: sometimes
e: yes, but only as related to military spending

49. Which government official is second in line of succession to the presidency?

a: vice president
b: governor
c: Speaker of the House
d: Secretary of State

50. Which government official is fourth in line of succession to the presidency?

a: vice president
b: governor
c: Speaker of the House
d: Secretary of State
e: Secretary of the Treasury

51. Which government official is fifth in line of succession to the presidency?

a: vice president
b: governor
c: Speaker of the House
d: Secretary of State
e: Secretary of the Treasury

52. In order to convict the President during an impeachment trial, this many senators must vote to do so:

a: 49
b: 51
c: 60
d: 67
e: 75

53. According to lecture, this is an example of interventionism "gone wild":

    a: Iran/Contra Gate
    b: Vietnam
    c: the black budget
    d: the international space station

54. American foreign policy has fluctuated between:

    a: the Monroe Doctrine and the Roosevelt Corollary
    b: a rock and a hard place
    c: compromise and inflexibility
    d: isolationism and interventionism

55. This scandal destroyed the Nixon Administration:

    a: Iran/Contra Gate
    b: the VietNam War
    c: the domino theory
    d: mutually assured destruction
    e: Watergate

56. How many members are there in the Electoral College, and how many votes does it take to become President of the United States (respectively)?

    a: 435/100   d: 535/269
    b: 535/100   e: 55/20
    c: 538/270

57. The candidate who did not receive the most popular votes became President of the United States in each of the following elections except:

    a: 2000   d: 1888
    b: 1876   e: 1932
    c: 1824

58. The only white demographic group that Obama "carried" in the 2008 presidential election was:

    a: 40–50-year-olds   c: 18–29-year-olds
    b: 15–20-year-olds   d: 55–65-year–olds

59. The Roosevelt Corollary to the Monroe Doctrine stated:
    a: "He who laughs last laughs joyfully"
    b: "Walk softly, and carry a big stick"
    c: "The enemy of my enemy is my friend"
    d: "Don't fire til you see the whites of their eyes"

60. This 1973 Congressional Act sought/seeks to curb the ascendancy of the "imperial presidency":
    a: Gulf of Tonkin Resolution
    b: Authorization for the Use of Military Force (AUMF)
    c: Bay of Pigs Acknowledgement
    d: War Powers Act
    e: Powell Doctrine

61. According to lecture, how much money did the U.S. spend on defense in the 1st five years of the Reagan presidency?
    a: $1 trillion   d: $10 billion
    b: $1 billion   e: $100 million
    c: $10 trillion

62. We must stop the spread of communism! I have described this foreign policy:
    a: Mutually Assured Destruction (MAD)
    b: We are the World's Police
    c: Let's drop the Iron Curtain
    d: the Domino Theory
    e: containment

63. American foreign policy has fluctuated between these two approaches:
    a: isolationism & interventionism
    b: isolationism & conservatism
    c: interventionism & containment
    d: containment & liberalism

64. Approximately how much money did Presidential candidate Barack Obama raise in his (2012) quest for re-election to the White House?
    a: $10 billion   d: $70 billion
    b: $700 million   e: $1 billion
    c: $700 billion

CHAPTER 6

Black Robes, White Robes

Image © Gary Blakeley, 2009. Used under license from Shutterstock, Inc.

American Jurisprudence

In order to fully comprehend our judicial system, it is important to review some of the fundamentals involved. Some of these fundamental realities apply to any aspect of the judiciary, whereas others have a more specific application. For example, the basic philosophy of American law is different from that of most European nations. The United States has what is called an adversarial system. This is where the primary motivation of parties in litigation is to win the proceedings, regardless of truth and/or justice. Conversely, many European countries have the inquisitorial system, where judges are not considered impartial arbiters, but truth-seekers. The debate about which system better ensures the most just outcome is far from over, and it is not germane to this text. However, it is crucial to understand that our adversarial system can work at its optimum only when the fact finder is an impartial arbiter.

The fact finder in our judicial system is going to be either a judge or a jury. The decision of which fact finder to have for legal proceedings is a choice that is left to the accused. Several of the amendments in the Bill of Rights require certain standards in our judicial system. Significantly, throughout the history of the American judiciary it is painfully clear that fact finders have frequently not been impartial arbiters. The ugly reality of bigotry in America cannot and should not be whitewashed. For instance, there have been long periods in our history during which women, the poor, and racial minorities were prohibited by law from serving on juries. There have also been many judges who wore black robes by day, and white robes by night. The real point is that the system is greatly threatened by biases of various sorts. As stated, our adversarial system loses its legitimacy when the fact finder is not a neutral arbiter. Specifically, many Americans expect a fair disposition, even if the circumstances do not lend themselves to a just outcome. The pretension that judges either have no biases, or have a superhuman ability to leave those biases outside of the courtroom, fuels a toleration of legalized institutional racism, sexism, and classism. There really is no magical training for judges that lifts them above the fray of a racially and economically polarized society such as America.

Additionally, the adversarial system has no workable response to the reality that a more skilled, better connected, and better prepared advocate enjoys a tremendous advantage. A point in case is the O. J. Simpson double murder trial. Most reviewers of the evidence in that case would say that the prosecution had an extremely strong circumstantial evidence case. Yet, Mr. Simpson was acquitted. Why? Simply put, he had the financial wherewithal to hire what was deemed the "Dream Team." Had that defendant not had deep pockets, he almost certainly would have been convicted. Admittedly, that is a simplification of the complexities of those legal proceedings, but the real point is that there are advantages and disadvantages to the adversarial system that are no small matters. This is because the impact (on the outcome) of fame, economic resources, and prosecutorial malfeasance is more the rule than the exception. The O. J. Simpson double murder trial was notorious, but something akin to a travesty of justice occurs regularly in our judicial system.

The Highest Court

Accordingly, this text will focus on the judges that we place our most supreme confidence in to be the necessary neutral arbiters of dispute. In a civil society, disputes that don't devolve into extralegal means are decided by courts of law. But, according to the concept of the separation of powers, courts are not to make, nor to enforce law. Courts are there to interpret the law, and this is a complex matter for many reasons. One reason for the complexity of law is that it derives from different sources. The supreme law of our land is the United States Constitution, but law can come from statutes, regulations, and even from judges themselves. Law that is made by judges based upon cases is known as common law. Common law is important because it is inextricably linked to a concept in American law known as *stare decisis*. This Latin term is roughly interpreted as "let the decision stand," and is the foundation of legal precedent. Stare decisis dictates that a decision that has been made in the same jurisdiction should be followed, except in extraordinary cases. Hence, a lower court in California must follow the decision of all relevant California Supreme Court cases if there are similar facts involved, and the matter is being decided according to state law. Also, a federal district court located in California must follow the decision of all relevant Ninth Circuit Court of Appeals cases if there are similar facts involved. Moreover, a Circuit Court of Appeals anywhere in the nation must follow the decision of all U.S. Supreme Court cases if there are similar facts involved. When different Circuit Courts of Appeals come to different decisions, even when there are similar facts involved the U.S. Supreme Court is likely to grant a writ of certiorari to clarify the legal inconsistency. Remember, under the system of federalism, although power is shared among the various states and the federal government, all persons are given the equal protection of the laws of this country. Therefore, the U.S. Supreme Court acts as a sort of adhesive to keep justice similar throughout the land. In this way our highest court have the final say on what is or is not allowable under the law.

This chapter on the Judiciary will focus on the U.S. Supreme Court for that very reason. Even though it has no enforcement powers, the prestige of the Court means that the legal precedence that it sets or keeps will be followed. Simultaneously, one must keep in mind that, as powerful as stare decisis is, legal precedence can be changed. Again, there are times when the Court gets ahead of public opinion, but for the most part the Court tries to stay in the mainstream. This is because not to do so would risk damage to the standing of the Court if it were to issue a ruling that the Executive Branch refused to enforce. Famously, in the 1832 case *Worcester v. Georgia,* when the Court held that Cherokee Indians were entitled to federal protection from state actions that infringed on their tribal sovereignty, President Jackson openly exclaimed his disdain. Referring to the Chief Justice, Jackson has been quoted as having said: "John Marshall has made his decision; now let him enforce it." There can be no doubt that the protection of Indian Rights was not popular in 19th Century America. In fact, the *Worcester* case ultimately made the Trail of Tears possible.

Nomination and Confirmation

The federal judiciary has judges on three levels, but regardless of the level, each of them serves under life tenure. Members of the federal bench are nominated by the President of the United States, but, unlike Cabinet members, they do not serve at the President's discretion. In fact, they do not serve at all if they are not confirmed by a simplemajority vote of United States senators. As related to Supreme Court nominations, this has happened only twelve times in American history. The last time the full Senate rejected a Supreme Court nominee was in 1987 with Judge Robert Bork.We will revisit Judge Bork's confirmation hearings as a watershed event that changed the confirmation process in a rather negative way. It may be astounding to some that, of the 179 current federal appellate judgeships, there is a near 50/50 split between those who were nominated by Democrat or Republican presidents. This fact could be expanded to include the justices who currently sit on the U.S. Supreme Court. This balance is essential because there is a profound effect of judicial appointments through the political process of Senate confirmation on the interpretation of law in the United States because political leanings influence judicial decisions.

Just as it is true that most judges (whether they be in the state or federal judicial system) have legal backgrounds traceable to prosecutorial law, it is also true that most Supreme Court justices have legal backgrounds traceable to the Circuit Courts of Appeals. The aforementioned fact means that the nomination process may be relatively quiet for federal judges, but the confirmation process is anything but that. Moreover, both the nomination and confirmation processes for openings on the Supreme Court have become a full blown media circus. This summer's nomination of the first Latina to the High Court is an example.

Judge Sonia Sotomayor was nominated with a largely unimpeachable, seventeen-year record as a jurist. She has obtained a rating of "well-qualified" by the American Bar Association. Yet, because of the political implications of a Supreme Court that will be more representative of the changing demographics of America, there were those who sought to impugn her character. In fact, when President Obama first announced her nomination, several white male conservative leaders went so far as to label her a racist. It did not take long for wiser heads in the Republican camp to realize that hurling invectives against this jurist with a longstanding record of upholding the rule of law was political suicide. Even though Elena Kagan had no experience as a jurist, her professional credentials were also largely unassailable. President Obama certainly (whether intentional or not) solidified his favor with the female electorate with these two choices. There was little doubt that these women would be confirmed, but the increased politicization of the confirmation process will be detailed later in this chapter.

Inner Workings

As a part of the unraveling of the mysteries of the U.S. Supreme Court, it is necessary to understand the basics of how the Court works. There are eight associate justices, and one Chief Justice. Each justice has several law clerks, and to "clerk" for the Court is a high honor in the legal profession. When the Court has decided to rule on a case, extensive legal research is done. Most of that research is done by the clerks, whom the justices then rely upon for what in the law is known as points and authorities. The only opportunity the general public has to participate in the proceedings is in the oral arguments for a case. If the United States is a party to, or has a vested interest in, the proceedings it will either have arguments made by the Solicitor General, or it may file what is known as an *amicus curiae* brief. This literally means "friend of the court." In order for a private attorney to make an oral argument before the Court, there are strict rules that must be followed. Merely having a license to practice law in the United States does not grant entitlement to argue a case before the highest Court.

Although there has been an increasingly loud cry to allow cameras in the Supreme Court over the years, most justices are against the practice. There is a legitimate concern of turning the highest Court into a media circus, with the Chief Justice as ringleader. On the other hand, openness is important in a democratic society, and reducing the mystery of the Court could increase and promote societal understanding of the function and operations of the pinnacle of our judicial system. It is possible for approximately 100 members of the general public to personally view Supreme Court oral arguments.

Once oral arguments are complete, the deliberations begin. This is done behind the secrecy of closed doors, and it is rare for any Justice to give a characterization of what takes place within those hallowed halls. The Justices take turns trying to convince each other of the legal merits of their perspectives. After deliberations, a vote is taken, and the majority side (if there is one) chooses who will author the Court's opinion.

There are a number of opinions that can be rendered. Sometimes there is a unanimous opinion. This is usually where the legal issues are rather clear, or where a matter of great import and impact has been decided. For example, the 1954 case, *Brown v. Board of Education,* was a unanimous opinion. It was important that the American public understand that the separate-but-equal doctrine was devoid of legal respectability. There are also *per curiam* opinions, which do not necessarily have to be unanimous. A per curiam opinion literally means "by the court," and it is rendered anonymously. Such decisions are rare. The aforementioned *Bush v. Gore* case was a per curiam opinion that was closely contested.

A plurality opinion is one where there was no point of view that received majority support. This is an important teaching tool because the fact that a Justice agrees with the decision in a case does not mean that the Justice agrees with the legal reasoning for the decision. That is why Justices write what are known as concurring opinions. A concurring opinion says, "I agree with the outcome, but I do not agree with your basis for the outcome." This occurs frequently. The reference to the outcome in a concurring opinion is to the majority opinion. The opposite of a concurring opinion is a dissenting opinion. A dissenting opinion says, "I disagree with the outcome, and here is why." Justices can write differing dissenting opinions for the same case for the same reasons that they can write differing concurring opinions.

Bork and Thomas Confirmation Hearings

It is not as if there had never been contentious confirmation hearings before the Senate Judiciary Committee, but in 1987, all the rules changed. In July of that year, then-President Ronald Reagan nominated former Solicitor General and sitting Circuit Court Judge Robert Bork for the Supreme Court. There was never a question raised about Judge Bork's qualifications for the job as far as his legal resume was concerned. However, within hours of the announcement, Senator Ted Kennedy strongly criticized the President's choice on the Senate floor. His description of Judge Bork's vision of America was alarming to many. As is true in any smear campaign, the truth is secondary to the charges leveled. The challenge to the Bork nomination was a purely political one. What was attacked were not his credentials, but his philosophy. Again, this was not the first time that this kind of challenge had been waged. Some decades earlier it was revealed that nominee Hugo Black was a member of the terrorist organization known as the Ku Klux Klan. But, he was allowed to join the Court anyway. The uniqueness of the Bork confirmation process is that the attacks actually worked. The nation witnessed the destruction of Judge Bork's character, and he was too pompous to mount an effective counterattack. Moreover, without supporting the approach, it is true that the perspectives of Judge Bork were (and still are) far outside of the mainstream. The details of Judge Bork's political demise can be discovered elsewhere, but the significance of the Bork confirmation hearings was that it changed the rules of the game in terms of who would be a likely nominee.

After Bork, Presidents sought nominees with scant judicial records, and untraceable personal flaws. Needless to say, since 1987 some of the presidential choices in nominees have ignored the lessons made available by the Bork fiasco.

The lack of adjustment began immediately with President Reagan. He followed up the Bork nomination with an announcement of his intention to nominate Douglas Ginsburg. Professor Ginsburg had to withdraw his candidacy even before being officially nominated, after it was revealed that he had smoked marijuana with some of his students at Harvard Law School.

In the curious case of Circuit Court Judge Clarence Thomas, the integrity of the confirmation process was placed before the American people. Judge Thomas was called upon in 1991 by President G.H.W. Bush to replace an icon in the struggle for civil rights. The fact that Judge Thomas is a Black man was little solace to those concerned about replacing a legal giant like Justice Thurgood Marshall. As the first Black man nominated to the highest Court, and a former Solicitor General, Justice Marshall had unimpeachable legal credentials, even without experience as a jurist. The notion that he would be replaced by a staunch conservative like Judge Clarence Thomas was a bitter pill for some to swallow. The avenue of attack of Thomas's nomination was a narrow one, because he had such a thin legal resume. He had been a Circuit Court Judge for only a little over a year, and he was wisely reluctant to espouse his political leanings during the confirmation hearing. That meant that a character assassination in the Bork tradition was in order. For days, the entire country became riveted as the charge of sexual harassment was made by a former subordinate, Law Professor Anita Hill. The lurid details of sexual invitations bolstered by pornographic material rivaled the daytime soap operas the confirmation hearing temporarily displaced. In the end, Judge Thomas survived the process without a recommendation from the Senate Judiciary Committee, which yielded a 7 to 7 vote. He survived a vote of the full Senate by a 52 to 48 margin. It was the closest successful confirmation in over a century. More importantly, it demonstrated that every federal judiciary confirmation would now be subject to the Bork treatment. A candidate's legal qualifications could easily become secondary to her or his personal viewpoints and behaviors. In other words, the process had become strikingly political.

The circumstance surrounding the confirmation of federal judges became so vitriolic that in 2005 when Republicans had control of the Senate, they threatened to use the "nuclear option" to prevent blocking tactics by Democrats. Democrats had effectively used the filibuster to prevent President G. W. Bush's federal judiciary nominees from getting a vote of the full Senate. The "nuclear option" refers to changing the Senate rules so that it takes only a simple majority to invoke cloture. In response to this threat, Democrats threatened to shut down the day-to-day operations of the Senate. On the eve of a Senate vote, there emerged a compromise led by the "Gang of Fourteen." These were seven Republicans, and seven Democrats who were able to convince their colleagues that the filibuster of judicial nominees would be used only in extreme cases, whatever that meant.

Although the crisis was averted, it remains a looming prospect because the nominees to the federal judiciary are crucial in their impact on legal interpretation. In any civil society, who is allowed to occupy the bench is of penultimate importance. If the federal judiciary is overrun with judges whose political leanings are outside of the mainstream, the implications are enormous. Too date, three of five federal judges serving today were nominated by Republican presidents.

In the summer and fall of 2005, President G. W. Bush also failed to get the message. Within weeks there had materialized two vacancies to the Court. The first was made possible by the announced retiring of the first woman to serve on the Court, Sandra Day O'Connor. The second was made possible by the death of Chief Justice William Rehnquist. Originally, Bush had nominated Circuit Court Judge John Roberts to replace Justice O'Connor, but he switched the nomination of Roberts to replace the Chief Justice position after Rehnquist's death. Bush then attempted to placate women's interest groups by nominating his crony, Harriet Miers, to replace Justice O'Connor. By nearly all accounts Ms. Miers was not qualified to sit on the Highest Court. When Republicans went public in criticizing his choice, Ms. Miers withdrew her nomination. There is little doubt that she would have been "Borked," whereas the quite conservative but well-qualified Roberts and Samuel Alito (the replacement candidate) were confirmed without much of a struggle.

Both of these justices are ideological conservatives, and it is folly to think that a judge checks her or his ideological leanings when she or he sits on the bench. In fact, there is a whole host of Supreme Court decisions that strongly indicate that bias has been integral to the decision-making process. Is there anyone who would argue against the fact that the most evil and vile racist attitudes prevailed in the holding of the 1857 *Dred Scott v. Sanford* case? How about the 1896 *Plessy v. Ferguson* case? Or, what about the 1944 *Korematsu v. United States* case? Perhaps now there can be a better understanding of the increasingly political tone of confirmation battles and hearings. We may be a nation of laws, and not of men, but it is men and women who interpret those laws.

Equal Protection Analysis

An area of great and continuing controversy in the American legal system is the notion of equal justice under the law. Arguably, the most significant sociopolitical movement in the history of the United States is the Civil Rights Movement. Civil rights are guaranteed according to status. Civil liberties are guaranteed to all, regardless of status. It can be quite confusing, but differentiate civil rights and civil liberties according to whether or not one is a citizen of the United States. Because civil liberties are all encompassing, this text will concentrate on them. The Bill of Rights, and the Fourteenth Amendment are the guideposts for the upholding of civil liberties in the United States. Citizens enjoy the protections in both parts of the Constitution. Noncitizens enjoy the protections of some parts. For example, there are certain rights that are considered fundamental, whether they are explicitly stated in the Constitution or not. The right to vote is a fundamental right, but it does not apply to noncitizens. The right to privacy is a fundamental right, and it applies to all persons. When there is a classification that causes a difference in treatment, it triggers an Equal Protection Analysis.

There are three tiers to the Analysis. If the classification touches upon the police power that states have to regulate health, morals, safety, or welfare, the Rational Basis Test is applied. If the classification touches upon gender, or time, place, and manner restrictions on free speech, Intermediate Scrutiny is applied. If the classification touches upon a fundamental right, or on "suspect" classifications such as race, Strict Scrutiny is applied.

The Rational Basis Test sets the standard that less than equal protection is allowable if the law or regulation is rationally related to an end that may be legitimately pursued by government.

Intermediate Scrutiny sets the standard that less than equal protection is allowable if the law or regulation is an important government interest that is furthered by substantially related means.

Strict Scrutiny sets the standard that less than equal protection is allowable if the law or regulation meets a three-pronged test. Prong one: Is the less than equal protection justified by a compelling government interest? Prong two: Is the law or regulation narrowly tailored to achieve that goal or interest? Prong three: Is the least restrictive means employed?

It is the Court that decides which Analysis will be used in a case. If your case is accorded the Rational Basis Review, you have the burden of proof, and you are likely to lose against the government regulation. If your case is accorded Intermediate Scrutiny, your chances are better because the government has the burden of proof. If your case is accorded Strict Scrutiny, the government has the burden of proof, and you are most likely to win against the government's conduct. Hence, how the Court decides to classify your case means everything to the prospect of whether or not you will prevail. The more conservative the make up of the Court, the less likely it will use Strict Scrutiny for its Equal Protection Analysis.

Hopefully, this has brought us full circle to understand that the confirmation process of federal judges in general, and of Supreme Court Justices in particular, has become a lightning rod for the political divisions in our society. The Constitution has enough "wiggle room" so that who it is who sits in judgment makes all the difference in terms of the outcomes of legal proceedings in the United States. If the Judiciary were truly neutral, the import and impact of who is on the bench would be greatly minimized, and we would not have irrefutable statistics that demonstrate a disparate impact on different groups.

Judicial Restraint and Judicial Activism

There are any number of philosophies of judicial interpretation, but the two major schools of thought are *judicial restraint* and *judicial activism*. For the most part, the more conservative jurists claim to be exercising judicial restraint, whereas the more liberal jurists are frequently accused of exercising judicial activism. These are by no means neat fits, however.

Judicial restraint is best described as an approach toward judicial interpretation that seeks primarily to do two things. One is to be extremely deferential to the acts of legislatures. The other is to be extremely deferential to the doctrine of *stare decisis*. To use a contemporary example, if a state legislature has passed a law that bans same-sex marriage, a judge exercising judicial restraint would most likely not delve into the rather obvious questions of the constitutionality of the law. This finding would have even firmer footing under the philosophy of judicial restraint if that jurisdiction had case law where a judge had determined that a ban on same sex marriage passes constitutional muster, so to speak. The major concern for adherents to judicial restraint is that judges should not legislate from the bench. This is a powerful notion, taking into account that there is no election of federal judges. Conversely, under our republican system of government, legislators are elected, and therefore have a greater claim to being the voice of the people's will. Hence, proponents of judicial restraint can invoke democracy itself as supporting their approach to judicial interpretation.

Analytically, there are significant problems with judicial restraint. Firstly, as far as respect for the actions of legislative bodies is concerned, it is not unusual for those bodies to impose the tyranny of the majority on others. In this country there is a long standing history of legislative bodies enacting the most pernicious of laws. Congress itself has enacted laws that have been racist, sexist, and classist. Many state legislatures have enacted laws that not only oppressed minorities, but that did so in a clearly unconstitutional manner. The Jim Crow laws of the South, North, East, and West come immediately to mind. If one were to follow the logic of the philosophy of judicial restraint, the merits of the laws enacted would fall subservient to the popularity of the laws enacted. That is not democracy, but democracy gone askew. Secondly, stare decisis cannot be allowed to be used as a bludgeon of oppression. In reviewing the most glaring example, where would America be today if the Warren Court had decided in the 1954 *Brown v. Board of Education,* and *Bolling v. Sharp* cases that the judicial precedence established in the 1896 *Plessy v. Ferguson* case should be respected? We would be lost in the evil wilderness of apartheid in this country. It is beyond question that stare decisis is one of the most important principles in American jurisprudence. The utility of following the judgments of courts throughout jurisdictions within the nation stabilizes our system, and provides a predictability whose value is inestimable. However, our society, like our world, is constantly evolving. If we either blindly follow stare decisis, or give it too much weight in its guidance, the result is inevitably destabilizing. As stated, judicial restraint is mostly adopted by those who adhere to conservative outlooks. Conservatism seeks either to keep something the same, or to roll something back to what it used to be. This is the practical and political equivalent of swimming upstream, or of trying to stop the rain. There is one irony to the conservative proponents of judicial restraint that is too irresistible to leave out. Every conservative member of the Court in the 2000 case *Bush v. Gore* violated the principles of judicial restraint, even though over the years they had repeatedly and loudly decried the legal analysis of some of their less conservative colleagues.

Judicial activism is best described as an approach toward judicial interpretation that seeks to primarily avoid miscarriages of justice under the notion of the Living Constitution. It is more difficult to define because it is largely, if not exclusively, used as a pejorative term. It is characterized as a method used by those who seek a specific outcome to a case. It is associated with personal bias, and it infers that its adherents usurp the separation of powers doctrine. The charge is that this is done either by legislating, or by making policy from the bench in contravention to democratic principles.

The reality is that, beyond the political posturing, all judges act in a manner consistent with both schools of thought. Judges are neither always exercising judicial restraint, nor are they always exercising judicial activism. Judicial interpretation mandates both approaches. What is really being exposed is the political nature of judging in a civil society. It is pretentious to claim, and ludicrous to believe, that judges are always neutral arbiters of disputes. That is not to say that judges don't attempt to be neutral in most cases, and to uphold the letter of the law. It is inescapable that, the higher the court, the more likely it will be making policy. Also, because the focus of this chapter is the federal judiciary and the United States Supreme Court, it is inevitable that the combination of the Supremacy Clause of the Constitution and the 1803 *Marbury v. Madison* case has imbued the Court with the power to overturn legislative acts, and to make policy. In other words, the Court cannot help but act in a manner consistent with both schools of thought. How one feels about the outcome means a great deal to whether the Court or judges are being judicially restrained, or are being judicially activist.

Strict Constructionism

Associated with either school of thought is strict constructionism. Erroneously there is a connotation of conservatism, but it simply means that, as a matter of judicial interpretation, the judge will look to the plain meaning of the text, and apply it as written. This is what most judges do, so strict constructionism should be considered as a mainstream approach in the American judicial system. However, it is not as simple as that because sometimes the plain meaning is not so plain. Our Constitution is a perfect example. There are numerous passages that must be left to judicial interpretation because there are several ways to read them. It should therefore be clear that strict constructionism is stale and robotic if it is applied to every circumstance. All reasonable jurists know that to be the case, so when there is ambiguity, they look to legislative intent and legislative history. A useful exercise for a student of political science is to review all the passages of the United States Constitution that are ambiguous. There is plenty to work with. One example would be the Necessary and Proper Clause. It is also known as the Elastic Clause. Is there any reasonable being who thinks that a strict constructionist approach to the Elastic Clause would yield a thoughtful result? The point is that judges must judge according to their training and wisdom. We trust that the referee isn't secretly rooting for one of the teams, but should we be blind in that trust just because we have been socialized not to question authority? What type of America would we live in today if the authority and legitimacy of judges (including the Supreme Court) is routinely accepted? The framers of the Constitution understood that there had to be room left for interpretation in order to meet the demands of an evolving society and world. Moreover, if there is no flexibility built into the Constitution to account for contemporary advances how relevant would our supreme law be today?

Recent Supreme Court Decisions

The last term of the U.S. Supreme Court has been a significant one that has confronted several "hot button" issues. The following review will cover Affirmative Action, DNA Testing of Arrestees, the Right to Remain Silent, Same Sex Marriage, and the Voting Rights Act. I have included the case citations to afford the reader the easy opportunity to read these cases first-hand. The treatment of each of these cases will include only the most pertinent facts, and the holdings.

Affirmative Action

The lastest U.S. Supreme Court foray into the murky world of affirmative action is mere further proof of the Court's incremental whittling away at what can at best be considered a dubious remedy for past discrimination. It is striking that the "backpeddling" on affirmative action mirrors the lack of resolve displayed during the immediate aftermath of the Civil War. From 1865 (starting point: end of Civil War) to 1877 (ending point: Hayes-Tilden Compromise) our nation started with the robust intention of incorporating the so-called "Freedmen" into American society. How preposterous to think that after 250 years of slavery, twelve years of Radical Reconstruction would be sufficient. How puny the American resolve to right such a gargantuan wrong.

From 1965 (starting point: passage of the Civil Rights, and Voting Rights Acts) to 1978 (ending point: the Bakke decision) our nation again started with the robust intention of incorporating the historically marginalized into American society. How preposterous to think that after 70 years of

Apartheid (starting point: the 1896 Plessy decision), allowing a small swath of Black people to enjoy the benefits all should enjoy could be realized through affirmative action. Again, how puny the American resolve to right the gargantuan wrong of racial segregation. The pattern is obvious. America does wrong; America feels bad; America proposes an inadequate remedy. The inadequate remedy is contorted into another alleged wrong. Today many consider affirmative action to be discrimination against white people. In the years following Reconstruction, many felt the need to reassert white supremacy. The ongoing vestiges of slavery and segregation are too evident to mention. After playing the game by skin color for centuries, who among us is so full of ignorance, hubris, or bigotry to argue that we are living in a post racial society where remedies based on race are not appropriate? Reparation has always been the most meaningful form of righting wrongs, especially if those wrongs have been economically impactful. If the discrimination was race based, why shouldn't the remedy be race based? As quiet as it is kept, the greatest beneficiaries of affirmative action policies have been white women.

Fisher v. University of Texas at Austin, 570 U.S. _____ (2013)

Petitioner Abigail Fisher ranked in the top 12% of her high school class. In 1997 Texas passed a Top 10% law [Texas Bill 588] that guaranteed admission to all state funded universities. Therefore, she did not qualify. Her Scholastic Aptitude Test (SAT) score was a slightly above average 1180. Her grade point average (GPA) was 3.59 on a 4.0 scale. Overall, her qualifications were comparable to other applicants, but the University of Texas (UT) testified that she would not have been admitted in any instance. On the District Court (trial) level UT's admissions plan was upheld. At the 5th Circuit Court of Appeals the District Court's decision was affirmed. On Monday, 24 June 2013 the U.S. Supreme Court "punted" by remanding the case back to the 5th Circuit in a 7-1 ruling. Justice Kagan recused herself due to her prior role as Solicitor General, and the lone dissenter was Justice Ginsburg. She stated that UT did its job by demonstrating that race-neutral approaches were insufficient to achieve diversity. In her dissent Justice Ginsburg cited *Grutter v. Bollinger*, 539 U.S. 306. Both Justices Scalia and Thomas wrote separate concurring opinions. Of significant note is that Justice Thomas (himself a beneficiary of affirmative action) proclaimed that he would have prohibited race as a consideration in all higher education admissions. The prevailing opinion was written by Justice Kennedy. He wrote: "Narrow tailoring also requires a reviewing court to verify that it is 'necessary' for the university to achieve the educational benefits of diversity."

DNA Testing of Arrestees

At some point in the near future, Americans are going to wonder what ever happened to the fundamental right known as the right to privacy. Our government rarely acts so boldly as to take it all in one fell swoop. The system of governance is designed around incrementalism. Because of this "slow drip" approach to draining the American people of their civil liberties, most will never miss the water until the well runs dry. A strong argument can be made for the DNA testing of those convicted of felonies, and a number of jurisdictions do. But arrestees? Literally thousands of Americans are arrested every year without formal charges being brought. Whatever happened to the presumption of innocence that is at the very heart of judicial fairness? Because privacy is classified as a fundamental right, courts are supposed to use the Strict Scrutiny Analysis. Has the 3 prong test mentioned earlier been met here? It must be supposed that the fear of criminal activity in the minds of Americans is paying great dividends to those who want to continue our inexorable slide into becoming a police state.

Maryland v. King, 569 U.S. _____ (2013)

On 3 June 2013 the Court rendered a 5-4 decision in this case. The alignment of the Justices was quite unusual. Again, Justice Kennedy (the most important swing vote on the Court) wrote the majority opinion. He likened DNA collection to fingerprinting and photographing, longstanding booking procedures when one is arrested. He was joined by Justices Alito, Breyer, Roberts, and Thomas. The dissenters: Justices Ginsburg, Kagan, Scalia, and Sotomayor. Justice Scalia wrote the dissenting opinion, and felt strongly enough that this procedure of DNA collection upon arrest is so violative of the reasonableness standard set forth in the 4th Amendment that he read a summary of the dissent from the bench.

Right to Remain Silent

Some may be quite surprised to learn that although the right to remain silent is codified in the U.S. Constitution 5th Amendment government prohibition against self incrimination, it was not until the time of the Civil Rights Movement that the U.S. Supreme Court outlawed heavy handed treatment of suspects by law enforcement. On 13 June 1966 the Court rendered its decision in *Miranda v. Arizona*, 384 U.S. 436 (1966). In part, the Court acknowledged the inherent coercive atmosphere of being held in custody. As a civil liberties protection, the Court directed that criminal suspects be advised of their 5th Amendment right not to incriminate themselves. On 17 June 2013 the Court moved farther away from protecting the rights of the accused through its latest decision on the right to remain silent.

Salinas v. Texas , 570 U.S. _____ (2013)

This was a 5-4 decision where the conservative majority prevailed, but it was a plurality opinion. This means that although five Justices supported the holding in the case, they did not do so for the same legal reasonings. The conservatives concluded that there is a difference between the Miranda fact that he was under custodial arrest, and the Salinas fact that he had voluntarily gone to the police station to answer questions. Suspect Salinas was asked to accompany the officers. In all likelihood, suspect Salinas felt as coerced in that police station as a person who had been brought there under arrest. If you have ever been questioned about a crime, and your potential involvement in said crime, in a police station you felt the inherent coercion of the atmosphere. But, let's not let reality get in the way of the Court's conclusion. Suspect Salinas had answered a number of questions, but when it came to answering a question about shotgun casings found at the murder scene, he "clammed up." At his trial, the prosecutors stated before the jury that his silence was evidence of his guilt. The Court determined that this proclamation before the jury was not violative of the right to remain silent.

It is not a baseless conclusion, but we should be clear about one thing. Should enough members of the general public be made aware of this decision, it will surely have a chilling effect on cooperation with law enforcement. By the Court's command, criminal suspects are better protected if they are arrested, than if they cooperate. It seems quite possible that an innocent individual could realize in the midst of police questioning that things are not going as well as being cooperative would have indicated. At that point many thoughtful and innocent people would fall silent. Should that be evidence of guilt? The tendency for most Americans is to understand these cases through the prism of an assumption of guilt, not innocence. In fact, Ernesto Miranda did rape the victim in his case. Does that mean that the confession that was beaten out of him should be admissible in an American court of law? Is it a stretch to think that many a suspect have been beaten by police, confessed, and recanted because they actually did not commit any crime whatsoever. Seem farfetched? Try doing a little research on false confessions, coercion, and the Innocence Project.

Same Sex Marriage

After years of avoidance, the Court took on two significant cases as related to equal rights for Gays and Lesbians. What some have hailed as the "Civil Rights Issue of Our Time", the movement of public opinion on same sex marriage over the last 10 years has been nothing short of amazing. One must be reminded that the right to marry in the United States is a fundamental right. Finally, the hollow recriminations about the sanctity of marriage, religious arguments about procreation, and other weak and constitutionally questionable certainly make one wonder: what took so long? It this issue resolved? Considering that both rulings had 5-4 margins, there is more to come on this topic. Considering the blatant "end around" of the Full Faith and Credit Clause, there is more to come on this topic. But, the momentum is clearly in the direction of accepting Gays and Lesbians as full members of American society. The Obama Administration's repeal of the absurd "Don't Ask, Don't Tell" embarrassment of the Clinton years has been progressive. And, yes, our military is still a soundly functioning apparatus of our government. It is disheartening that less than 20 years ago Congress would have the temerity to pass the Defense of Marriage Act (DOMA). Although former President Clinton went public earlier this year with his support of the repeal of DOMA, what does it say about him that he signed the bill in the first place? Is his signing on justifiable because DOMA passed by veto proof margins?

The repeal of DOMA in total is what needs to happen at this point. In the California Proposition 8 case, the Court receives kudos for the artfulness of the dodge. But the Court did not go "too far, too fast," because it did not declare a fundamental right to same sex marriage nationwide.

United States v. Windsor, 570 U.S. (2013)

Edith Windsor and Thea Spyer were lovers for over 40 years. In 2007, these residents of New York became legally married in Canada. In 2009, Thea Spyer died, having left her sizeable estate to Edith Windsor. Due to the restrictions in DOMA, Edith Windsor was required by the federal government to pay over $363K in estate taxes. Had their marriage been legally recognized, she would have had to pay no taxes. Ms. Windsor won in federal district court, won in the 2nd Circuit Court of Appeals, and has now won in the U.S. Supreme Court by the narrowest 5-4 ruling. Her estate taxes have been returned, and Section 3 of DOMA has been declared unconstitutional. On 26 June 2013 once again, Justice Kennedy (the all important swing vote) authored the majority opinion. He was joined by

Justices Breyer, Ginsburg, Kagan, and Sotomayor. He characterized Section 3 of DOMA: "as a deprivation of the equal liberty of persons that is protected by the Fifth Amenment."

But, what about Section 2 of DOMA? It reads: "No State, territory, or possession of the United States, or Indian tribe, shall be required to give effect to any public act, record, or judicial proceeding of any other State, territory, possession, or tribe respecting a relationship between persons of the same sex that is treated as a marriage under the laws of such other State, territory, possession, or tribe, or a right or claim arising from such relationship." How does this "square" with the Full Faith and Credit Clause of the U.S. Constitution, Article IV, Section 1? Puzzling to think that the 5th Amendment to the U.S. Constitution should be respected, but the Constitution itself (Art. IV, Section 1) should not.

Hollingsworth v. Perry, 570 U.S. (2013)

Proposition 8 in California amended the state constitution to declare marriage as only between a man and a woman. This was by popular vote (through ballot initiative) in a state that for a century has developed direct democracy. In federal district court, Judge Vaughn Walker (himself a gay man) declared Proposition 8 unconstitutional on the merits. The 9th Circuit Court of Appeals affirmed. On 26 June 2013 the U.S. Supreme Court held that the defenders of Proposition 8 lacked appellant standing to bring the case. Because the Court decided that the 9th Circuit heard the case in error (because the defenders of Proposition 8 lacked standing there also), this virtually allowed Judge Walker's findings to be the final word on this matter. Even though this was also a 5-4 decision, there was a strikingly strange alignment in this case. Chief Justice Roberts authored the majority opinion, which sidestepped the true issues set forth in the District Court. Judge Walker used a Rational Basis Test Analysis to conclude that Proposition 8 was in violation of the Due Process, and Equal Protection Clauses of the 14th Amendment. Because the Court did not reach the substantive merits of the case, the ruling does not apply to same sex marriage bans in states other than California. Chief Justice Roberts was joined by Justices Breyer, Ginsburg, Kagan, and Scalia.

Voting Rights

It would take a deft arguer to successfully convince Americans that there is a more sacred right than the right to vote. In a representative democracy, no more fundamental right other than freedom itself can possibly exist. It is for that precise reason that the struggle over the right to exercise the franchise has been heated, and ongoing. The lines are rather clearly drawn. Legislative and judicial measures that tend to suppress the vote are supported by most Republicans. Conversely, legislative and judicial measures that tend to extend the vote to more Americans are supported by most Democrats. This is due to the fact that Republicans are a minority political party in America. The more efforts that are made to get people to the polls, the lesser the chances for a Republican candidate's victory. Of course there are exceptions to these general truths, but the record is clear. What is disturbing is the reluctance on the part of some Americans to face this reality of voter suppression. It is no different than racism. Just because the overwhelming majority of racists don't openly declare their narrow-mindedness doesn't mean racism doesn't exist, or is no longer a potent force of discrimination and benefit distribution in our modern society. Similarly, just because the overwhelming majority of those who seek to undermine the sacred and fundamental right of voting don't openly declare it doesn't mean those people/forces don't exist. Just a few decades ago, the methods of voter suppression were much more crude. Polling taxes, literacy tests, lynchings, beatings, etc., were the preferred tools of the trade. Today, it is gerrymandering, requirements of photographic identifications, defective voting machinery, inadequate numbers of polling places, etc.

The Voting Rights Act that was passed and signed in 1965 is the crown jewel of civil rights in this country. On four separate occasions, Congress has voted to reauthorize the Voting Rights Act. The more that we as a society pretend that we have reached the "promised land" of racial discrimination as a past problem, the more we are doomed to the very opposite of domestic tranquility. Admittedly, America is suffering from "racial fatigue". But the only reason we are so tired of this seemingly intractable problem is because we have not been aggressive enough in combating it. Half hearted measures like affirmative action are no remedy for our legacy of racism. Halfhearted proclamations like "America's no longer racist, after all we have a Black president!" are wholly inadequate for the American who has to wait in line for hours to cast a vote in Cleveland, or Miami, or some location in Texas, Alabama, Mississippi, or the like.

Shelby County, Alabama v. Holder, 570 U.S. _____ (2013)

On 25 June 2013 in a 5-4 decision authored by Chief Justice Roberts, the Court ruled Section 4(b) of the Voting Rights Act of 1965 unconstitutional. The District (trial) court upheld the constitutionality of Section

4(b), as did the U.S. Court of Appeals for the D.C. Circuit. Section 4(b) deals with the coverage formula that is closely connected with the pre-clearance part of the law that can be found in Section 5. With the holding that Section 4(b) is unconstitutional, and therefore no longer useable, the Section 5 preclearance portion is a toothless tiger. In effect, this decision gutted the Voting Rights Act. Notably, Justice Thomas in a concurring opinion that evinces his never ending dark quest to "out conservative the conservatives" stated that he would also invalidate Section 5. Ignoring the fact that Congress made a number of findings in reauthorizing the Voting Rights Act in 2006, the majority pointed to the fact that the coverage formula included the very same jurisdictions from the original law. For a Chief Justice, and a conservative majority that frequently lean on the notion of being deferential to Congress, this decision is rank. Joining the Chief Justice were Justices Alito, Kennedy, Scalia, and Thomas. It is rare and ironic that the Court would overturn legislation so thoroughly considered by Congress. It must also be emphasized that the Voting Rights Act has enjoyed tremendously strong bipartisan support in Congress. For the record, the reauthorization vote in 2006: House = 390–33; Senate = 98–0.

It is also rare and ironic that the Court would overturn legislation that is specifically empowered by the U.S. Constitution. The 15th Amendment expressly authorizes Congress to enforce fair voting measures. America fantasizes about a post racial society, but it is nothing more than a wet dream. Until the benefits and detriments (and that includes the intergenerational benefits and detriments) of having a certain color of skin are removed post racialism will only destabilize American society. No justice, no peace.

Conclusion

The focus of this chapter has been the federal judiciary, and the United States Supreme Court. But, most of the average citizens' interaction with the judicial system happens in state court, and begins with a law enforcement officer. The recent arrest of the nation's eminent African American scholar, and the aftermath of that debacle, keeps open the debate about the role of legal interactions in our everyday lives. It is refreshing to hear a President of the United States echo the sentiments of the victims of inequitable treatment in our society.Dr.Gates was arrested in his own home and charged with some nonsense about disorderly conduct. The fact that the charges were dropped within days of the outcry about this abuse of process is welcomed, but how many other Black, Brown, or poor men have been unjustly arrested and charged without the benefit of high social standing and notoriety? Even more recently, the question must be put: How many of you would feel that justice were served if Trayvon Martin were a person you cared about? Remember, the "Stand Your Ground" laws are public policy set forth by fearful, bigoted, and misguided elements within our society. Exploring the implications of the role of the judiciary in setting public policy is a worthy inquiry that goes beyond this guide, but that is not overlooked by it. It is more apparent in reviewing the judicial branch of the American government than in examining either Congress or the Presidency that a postracial America remains a lofty goal, but nothing more than a pipedream. The deflection of questions about the neutrality of judges, and the systematic and institutional racism, sexism, and classism that bedevil American legal proceedings are ineffectual in building a civil society where justice is truly blind, instead of the lady who peeks beyond the blindfold to see what color your skin is, or whether you are a male or female, or rich or poor.

Chapter 6
Study Guide

1. If a woman alleges an equal protection violation based on gender, courts will use this analysis:

   a   stare decisis
   b: police power

   c: intermediate scrutiny
   d: strict scrutiny

2. The power of judicial review comes from:

   a: executive agreements
   b: the Constitution
   c: the case of *Marbury v. Madison*
   d: the Bill of Rights
   e: natural rights

3. Punishment is _____ for whites than for minorities convicted of the same crime.

   a: scarier
   b: less severe
   c: funnier

   d: harsher
   e: the same

4. Paid advertising can be constitutionally protected as a form of:

   a: symbolic speech
   b: exempted speech

   c: private speech
   d: commercial speech

5. The Exclusionary Rule was first extended to state court proceedings in the Supreme Court case of:

   a: *Nix v. Williams*
   b: *Miranda v. Arizona*

   c: *Betts v. Brady*
   d: *Mapp v. Ohio*

6. Nearly _____ % of all criminal cases are resolved by plea bargaining.

   a: 1%
   b: 11%
   c: 90%

   d: 50%
   e: 25%

7. The burning of an American flag in a peaceful protest is an example of:

    a: a protected action under the symbolic speech concept
    b: a violation of the Constitution
    c: a protected action under the clear and present danger concept
    d: an issue not yet decided by the Supreme Court

8. I am alleging that my fundamental rights have been violated by the government. If I cite the 14th Amendment, courts will use this analysis:

    a: stare decisis   c: intermediate scrutiny
    b: police power   d: strict scrutiny

9. The Exclusionary Rule prohibits:

    a: defendants from testifying in their own behalf
    b: a spouse from testifying in a criminal case
    c: improperly obtained evidence from being used by prosecutors
    d: a spouse from testifying in a civil case
    e: self incrimination

10. The effect of *Plessy v. Ferguson* on racial segregation was to establish a:

    a: "clear and present danger" principle to further integration
    b: pattern to outlaw segregation in the South
    c: pattern for racial integration throughout the country
    d: constitutional cornerstone of racial discrimination throughout the country

11. The Establishment Clause deals with which Amendment, based on which civil liberty?

    a: 1st/freedom of religion   c: 4th/right to privacy
    b: 2nd/right to bear arms   d: 5th/right to due process

12. According to the "clear and present danger" test:
    a: a speech must be unclear as to its intent for it to be ruled unconstitutional
    b: the action called for must be constitutionally "vague" in order to be ruled unconstitutional
    c: free speech may not be curbed, because speech alone cannot bring about action
    d: free speech may not be curbed, because we live in America
    e: free speech can be curbed if such speech would cause a condition that Congress has the power to prevent

13. The *Roe v. Wade* case decided the abortion issue on the basis of:
    a: right to privacy   c: freedom of speech
    b: freedom of religion   d: gender

14. On what basis did a federal judge rule parts of Proposition 187 unconstitutional in 1995?
    a: only the federal government has authority over immigration
    b: stare decisis
    c: welfare benefits are for everyone
    d: English cannot be the official language where the majority of the people are not English

15. The Equal Pay Act of 1963 has:
    a: only applied when women and men do exactly the same job
    b: never been enforced
    c: only applied to comparable worth situations
    d: totally equalized pay between women and men

16. Gag orders are:
    a: designed to eliminate illegal speech
    b: designed to eliminate unlawful assembly
    c: part of the controversy over the death penalty
    d: restrictions on publications of news concerning pretrial hearing or trials in progress

17. How can the Supreme Court check/balance the President or Congress?
    a: through judicial review   c: it can not
    b: through legal enforcement   d: through public opinion

18. Sexual harassment of women in the workplace is:
    a: no longer prohibited by statute
    b: prohibited by Title VII of the Civil Rights Act of 1964
    c: considered a form of reverse discrimination against men
    d: considered "protective" legislation that the Supreme Court has ruled unconstitutional

19. Public officials may sue for libel if they can prove the statement:
    a: was false
    b: hurt the official's reputation
    c: hurt the official's feelings
    d: was made with actual malice
    e: was true

20. The view that most of the protections of the Bill of Rights are included under the Fourteenth Amendment's protection against state government is called the:
    a: necessary and proper theory
    b: inclusionary theory
    c: nullification theory
    d: incorporation theory
    e: low end theory

21. The Dred Scott case:
    a: contributed to making the Civil War inevitable
    b: provided full citizenship for all African Americans
    c: freed the slaves in the South
    d: contributed to a more peaceful resolution to the slavery issue

22. When we are speaking of civil liberties, we are referring to limitations on government as outlined in the:
    a: Madisonian Model
    b: Declaration of Independence
    c: Articles of Confederation
    d: Magna Carta
    e: Bill of Rights

23. The requirement of the issuance of a warrant (based on probable cause) to search can be found in the _____ Amendment to the U.S. Constitution.
    a: 1st
    b: 2nd
    c: 3rd
    d: 4th
    e: 5th

24. The Confrontation Clause deals with which Amendment, based on which civil liberty?

    a: 6th/right to cross examine   c: 4th/right to privacy
    b: 2nd/right to bear arms   d: 5th/right to due process

25. Stare decisis is a doctrine:

    a: enabling court decisions to vary from case to case
    b: providing guidance to judges when common law does not apply
    c: encouraging the following of precedent or previous court decisions
    d: requiring hearings about complaints arising from regulations

26. The level of trial courts in the federal judiciary hierarchy is the:

    a: district courts   c: Supreme Court
    b: Circuit Court of Appeals   d: state courts

27. The justices who believe that the Court should use its power to alter or challenge the policy direction of Congress, state legislatures, or administrative agencies are advocating:

    a: judicial restraint   c: strict constructionism
    b: judicial activism   d: moderate pragmatism

28. The courts that have become "stepping stones" to appointment to the Supreme Court are the:

    a: District Courts   c: Circuit Courts of Appeal
    b: State Supreme Courts   d: Tax Court

29. Appellate jurisdiction means the authority of a court to:

    a: serve as a trial court
    b: hear cases for the first time
    c: review decisions from a lower court
    d: establish grand juries

30. A writ of certiorari is issued by the Supreme Court only when:

    a: a majority of justices vote for such a request
    b: four justices vote for such a request
    c: a unanimous Court supports such a request
    d: the Solicitor General approves such a request

31. A Justice who accepts the majority decision, but not the reasons for it may write his/her own:

    a: minority opinion   c: amicus curiae opinion
    b: majority opinion   d: concurring opinion

32. The official who represents the national government in the Supreme Court is the:

    a: Attorney General   c: Vice-President
    b: Solicitor General   d: Chief Justice

33. In terms of enforcement powers, the Supreme Court:

    a: has now acquired its own police force
    b: relies upon the good will of the public to see that its decisions are enforced
    c: does not make decisions that have to be enforced
    d: must rely on other units of government to carry out its decisions

34. The U.S. Supreme Court overturning the Florida Supreme Court over vote counting in the 2000 Presidential election surprised many observers because:

    a: of judicial review
    b: of support of civil rights cases
    c: of support of rights of accused cases
    d: of support of states' rights cases

35. Because of the supremacy clause the states cannot:

    a: deny citizens of another state the same privileges and immunities they extend to their own citizens
    b: discriminate against citizens from another state
    c: use their reserved or concurrent powers to thwart national policies
    d: tax their citizens beyond national governmental rates
    e: institute an official religion

36. The constitutional concept of police powers is created by the:

    a: interstate commerce clause   d: combined power clause
    b: necessary and proper clause   e: supremacy clause
    c: 10th Amendment

37. What argument did the U.S. Supreme Court embrace in their infamous decision in *Bush v. Gore* (2000)?

    a: judicial review   c: voter fraud
    b: an equal protection violation   d: conservatism

38. Law that is made by judges is also known as:

    a: judicial restraint   d: jurisdiction
    b: judicial economy   e: common law
    c: bad precedent

39. O. J. Simpson was acquitted in criminal court, yet held liable in civil court due to the:

    a: Crackerbarrel Doctrine
    b: Sustained Responsibility Doctrine
    c: Stare Decisis Doctrine
    d: Separate Sovereignty Doctrine

40. The majority of arrests today involve:

    a: murder   c: federal crimes
    b: drug offenses d: white collar crimes

41. The current U.S. Supreme Court has:

    a: 5 Independents and 4 Democrats
    b: 2 Democrats and 7 Republicans
    c: 4 Republicans and 3 Democrats
    d: 4 Democrats, 4 Republicans, and 1 Independent
    e: 5 Republicans and 4 Democrats

42. Which U.S. Supreme Court case overturned the separate-but-equal doctrine?

    a: *Brown v. Bd. of Education*   d: *Korematsu v. U.S.*
    b: *Plessy v. Ferguson*   e: *Mapp v. Ohio*
    c: *Dred Scott v. Sandford*

43. Which of the following inalienable (fundamental) rights is not explicitly stated in the U.S. Constitution?

    a: gun ownership   c: liberty
    b: privacy   d: protecting property

44. Both the U.S. and California constitutions prohibit involuntary servitude except:

    a: for Blacks
    b: for illegal aliens
    c: to punish crime
    d: to pay debts

45. A technically incorrect search warrant can be legal under the concept of:

    a: the "good faith" exception
    b: the Miranda rule
    c: the unreasonable search and seizure
    d: the right to an attorney if you cannot afford one

46. Most of the protections found in the Bill of Rights:

    a: apply only to the national government
    b: have been extended by the Supreme Court to be applicable at the national and state levels
    c: apply only to the state governments
    d: none of the above

47. The wall of separation between church and state is best found in what clause of the U.S. Constitution?

    a: the free exercise clause
    b: the establishment clause
    c: the equal protection clause
    d: the wall of separation clause
    e: the elastic clause

48. What were the Alien and Sedition Acts?

    a: laws passed in the 1790s that made it a crime to say or publish anything that would defame the government of the United States
    b: laws that made it a crime for foreign immigrants to belong to the Communist Party or other anti-American organizations
    c: a law passed by Congress denying property rights to all non-citizens
    d: laws passed during the Civil War denying Confederate sympathizers the right of free speech

49. In the realm of the Judiciary, ADR stands for:

    a: automatic determination of rights
    b: alternative dispute resolution
    c: attention deficit review
    d: all defendant's rights

50. Law that is made by legislatures/judges is also known (respectively) as:

    a: statutory/civil law
    b: commoner/civilian law
    c: judicial/natural law
    d: jurisdiction
    e: civil/common law

51. Why is it always better to plead nolo contendere instead of guilty?

    a: because of the lower burden of proof in a civil court
    b: because Latin sounds sexy
    c: because of double jeopardy
    d: because of the higher burden of proof in a civil court

52. The right to sue and the power of a court to hear a suit are also known by these legal terms (respectively):

    a: standing/jurisdiction
    b: standing/sitting
    c: civil liberties/jurisdiction
    d: jurisdiction/standing
    e: de novo/stare decisis

53. The level of trial courts in the state/federal judiciary hierarchy (respectively) is the:

    a: superior/district courts
    b: Circuit Court of Appeals
    c: Supreme Court
    d: inferior/superior courts
    e: municipal/superior courts

54. Each of the following will enable suit to be brought in federal court except:

    a: a federal question is involved
    b: diversity jurisdiction exists
    c: the federal government is a party
    d: an advisory opinion is sought
    e: there is a habeas corpus petition involved

55. Is a line item veto constitutional?

    a: yes
    b: no
    c: maybe
    d: sometimes
    e: yes, but only as related to military spending

56. What is the meaning of stare decisis?
    a: let the decision stand
    b: look the devil in the eye
    c: be confident in the rule of law
    d: the body is stiffening

57. Which of the following *is not* a source of law?
    a: U.S. Constitution
    b: statutes
    c: common law
    d: law enforcement
    e: case law

58. The definition of a civil society is one where:
    a: there is the rule of law
    b: there is the rule of thumb
    c: there is the rule of 4
    d: there is the rule of might

59. According to lecture, the judiciary is divided into these four realms:
    a: constructionist/activist/obstructionist/practical
    b: state/federal/civil/criminal
    c: district/supreme/state/federal
    d: liberal/conservative/left/right

60. Which 4 Amendments to the U.S. Constitution detail the rights of the accused?
    a: 1/2/3/4
    b: 2/3/4/5
    c: 3/4/5/6
    d: 4/5/6/8
    e: 7/8/9/10

61. What was the basis cited by the California Supreme Court when in 2009 it ruled that same sex marriage should be again declared illegal?
    a: DOMA
    b: state law, as approved by the voters in 2008
    c: stare decisis
    d: fags are a drag
    e: dikes I don't like

62. All of the following are exceptions to the warrant requirement except:
    a: hot pursuit
    b: cold pursuit
    c: evanescence
    d: consent
    e: automobile

63. Which of the following types of vetoes have been ruled unconstitutional?

    a: veto   d: executive veto
    b: pocket veto   e: overridden veto
    c: line item veto

64. The USA Patriot Act (at least parts thereof) is probably unconstitutional because of which Amendment?

    a: 2nd   d: 5th
    b: 3rd   e: 6th
    c: 4th

65. The U.S. Supreme Court cases *McCulloch v. MD* & *Gibbons v. Ogden* involved which constitutional clauses? (respectively)

    a: Fugitive Slave Clause & Privileges and Immunities Clause
    b: Necessary and Proper Clause & Commerce Clause
    c: Bear Clause & Santa Clause
    d: Santa Clause & Commerce Clause

66. Which of the following amendments does not involve civil rights and liberties:

    a: 1st   d: 14th
    b: 4th   e: 19th
    c: 27th

67. This 2010 Supreme Court case declared it unconstitutional for Congress to limit the amount of money a corporation or union could contribute to an election campaign:

    a: *Kelo v. New London*   d: *U.S. v. Nixon*
    b: *Buckley v. Valeo*   e: *Citizens United v. FEC*
    c: *Potter v. Stewart*

68. Which of the following is not a component of the 8th Amendment to the U.S. Constitution:

    a: no excessive fines
    b: no excessive bails
    c: due process
    d: no cruel or unusual punishment

69. Which of the following amendments does not involve the rights of the accused?

a: 1st
b: 4th
c: 8th
d: 6th
e: 5th

70. The Takings Clause (Eminent Domain) of the 5th Amendment to the U.S. Constitution was given questionable interpretation (Public Use) in which Supreme Court case?

a: *Dred Scott v. Sandford*
b: *Lemon v. Kurtzman*
c: *Citizens United v. Federal Election Commission*
d: *Terry v. Ohio*
e: *Kelo v. New London*

71. Which of the following areas of legislation is not included in the powers accorded to states by the 10th Amendment?

a: health
b: safety
c: morals
d: welfare
e: economics

72. Which of the following is not one of the 3 tiers of analysis as related to Equal Protection (14th Amendment)?

a: strict scrutiny
b: intermediate scrutiny
c: close scrutiny
d: rational basis test

73. The strongest argument for the unconstitutionality of the Defense of Marriage Act (DOMA) is:

a: religion
b: freedom of religion
c: equality
d: the Commerce Clause
e: the Full Faith and Credit Clause

74. American Jurisprudence is based upon which system?

a: capitalism
b: democracy
c: adversarial
d: inquisitorial
e: integrated democracy

75. What percentage of current federal judges were appointed by Republican/Democrat presidents (respectively)?

a: 75/25
b: 62/38
c: 25/75
d: 90/10
e: 10/90

CHAPTER 7

A More Perfect Union

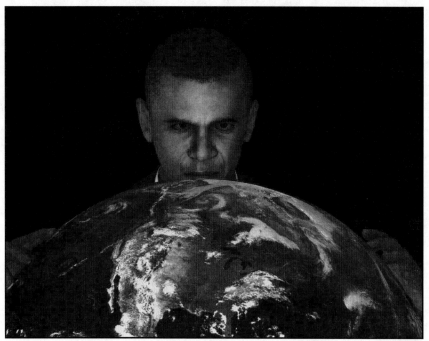

Image © Jeffrey Collingwood, 2009. Used under license from Shutterstock, Inc.

The Role of Government

It is not surprising that, over two hundred years after the founding of the American republic, deep divisions remain over the role of government in our lives. On the traditional political spectrum, there are the opposite poles of left and right. Most observers consider the left pole of the spectrum to be liberal, and the right pole of the spectrum to be conservative. As a matter of ideology, most Americans are closer to the center of the spectrum than to either pole. It is oxymoronic that many who argue for a diminished role of government in our lives also claim to be in lockstep with the ideals of the founders of this body politic. Those who adhere to the political ideology of the far right of the political spectrum (e.g., libertarians) vociferously claim to be greater patriots, but are these perspectives in accord with the Constitution? Those who adhere to the political ideology of the far left of the political spectrum (e.g., communists) also make their claims, but how do their claims measure up to the ideals expressed by the founders through the Constitution? There are measurements that can be analyzed that could prove helpful in responding to these queries.

The Preamble to the United States Constitution lists several basic objectives of the American government. A "more perfect union" is the first listed. To "establish justice" is the second listed. To "insure domestic tranquility" is the third listed. To "provide for the common defence" is the fourth listed. To "promote general welfare" is the fifth listed. And, to "secure the blessings of liberty" is the last listed in the Preamble. Although not explicitly stated as the role of government, it is reasonable to conclude that the six objectives listed provide a template for the role of government.

Within the first decades following ratification of the Constitution and the Bill of Rights, our government embarked on making the noble ideals of the Preamble into reality for Americans. The massive undertaking of living up to the ideals in the Preamble continues to this day. Whether it is more likely that we can continue to form a more perfect union without a significant role for government is a raging debate and division in modern-day America. It seems that the likelihood of meeting the objectives of the Preamble increases exponentially with a greater role for government. The complexity of an integrated global economy that is constantly evolving due to technological "advances" requires a greater role for government. Although this is unsettling for large swaths of the American populace, it is an inescapable reality that some problems are impossible to resolve without government intervention and assistance. There is a well-established pattern that, when the federal government is tepid in its approach to major challenges, the entire society suffers. A recent example is that the federal government's failure (by the G. W. Bush administration) to acknowledge the economic recession that began in 2007 hampered serious efforts to take countermeasures to the crisis that ensued.

Another example would be race relations. In the Preamble, the language reads plainly, "establish justice." Taking into account the advantage of hindsight, few would argue today that the federal intervention in passing civil rights legislation over forty years ago yielded worse race relations. Moreover, it is not without merit to argue that the Civil Rights Movement, and the role of the federal government in supporting that movement (albeit late) resulted in furthering every single objective of the Preamble.

The role of government is not really a matter of whether, but to what degree. It is beyond question that Americans have grown quite skeptical of their government. It is also beyond question that Americans expect their government to solve the problems of the day. If the critique would focus on how to develop a more responsive government instead of viewing the government as the enemy of the people, a more perfect union would surely follow.

The national election results in November 2008 and 2012 portend a psychological realignment for the American body politic. Although there is some merit to the argument that America is a basically conservative society, a political shift has begun. It is not as much a shift from the right pole of the political spectrum to the left pole of the political spectrum as it is a shift from left and right to the center. This has created a tremendous opportunity for American society. When the American people perceive that the federal government is effective and responsive to their needs, the role of government will increase in a welcome way. The election of President Obama raised political expectations for many Americans. It is apparent that President Obama feels the pressure of those expectations, which is why his approach to the major challenges of the day seems so ambitious. The culture of this country is not accommodating to a patient approach. The irony is that, as the president, despite his message of change, Mr. Obama inevitably has to defend aspects of our political system and culture that are truly indefensible. The author of a political science text is not so bound.

Activism

The political history of the United States is replete with examples of how effective an active, and politically participatory society can be to bring about change. There is no reason to "reinvent the wheel." When Americans become serious about forming a more perfect union we will have one. It is of extreme importance to realize that every progressive social movement in American history was initially opposed by the American government. Think about it; the abolition of slavery took over a century of agitation. It took a bloody, divisive Civil War, but eventually the government got on the right side of history. The right for women to vote took decades of agitation. It took the ratification of the 19th Amendment, but eventually the government got on the right side of history. The Civil Rights Movement took decades of agitation. It took the passage of several significant pieces of legislation, but eventually the government got on the right side of history. The right to vote for eighteen- year-olds is probably the most illustrative case in point. In less than a decade the contradiction of the government being able to compel an eighteen year old to die in military conflict, while eighteen-year-olds could not vote for those who were compelling them to die via military draft was resolved with the ratification of the 26th Amendment in 1971. In less than 5 years activism forced change. The same can be true for the circumstances of today. The key to it all is to organize. The challenge for today is to have those who are activists, could become activists, or have been activists realize that in order to effectively organize there must be a hierarchy. The promotion of anarchy, with its distaste for organized, hierarchical structure is a double edged sword that is extremely counterproductive to forming a more perfect union. One edge of that sword is the reactionary, cynical, destructive, opportunistic element within the philosophy of anarchism. The other edge of that sword is the undermining notion that all hierarchical structures are inherently bad and oppressive. It should not be inferred that every time a public demonstration results in the destruction of public and/or private property that anarchists are to blame. In some instances it is just disaffected youth who are the transgressors. Those of us who have worked in community based organizations know how damaging to the cause even a small percentage of those who seek to release their frustrations and negativity can be. Strong leadership, strong organizations, and disciplined training can neutralize this counterproductive behavior.

An example of the above are two political "rumblings" that are misnomered as movements, but have yet to establish themselves as such. The Occupy and Tea Party "Movements" are crisp proof of the need for identifiable leadership, and organizational discipline and structure. The term movement is used loosely here because a key feature of a political movement is duration. "Occupy" caught fire and sizzled out in relatively short order. "Tea Party" has shown more endurance, but the sustainability it takes to aptly call it a movement has yet to be evidenced. Both Occupy and the Tea Party must resolve their inherent contradictions. For Occupy they seek change from the same government that created and perpetuates the conditions they fight against. Benevolent, compassionate, responsible capitalism is the equivalent of putting lipstick on a pig and marveling at the swine's beauty. For the Tea Party, its reactionary ideology has broad appeal, but will continue to deteriorate into a twisted combination of conservatism, libertarianism, and populism that has little chance of becoming anything more than a fringe element in American politics. The "Tea Partiers" have found their greatest refuge in the ultra right wing of the Republican Party, which is the political equivalent of nowheresville. This is not to say that they lack influence. In fact, the Tea Party wing of Republicans is a driving force of the Republican agenda. That is not good news for a political party that is losing national traction in the face of an inevitable demographic shift.

It is unavoidable that those who seek to ignore history are doomed to repeat it. The template for forming a more perfect union through activism is clear. The younger generations of Americans would be well served to delve deeper into that history of the development and effectiveness of social movements. It is only then that youthful vigor can supplant deeply rooted hypocrisies. As a child of the 60s it is not difficult for me to know what can be accomplished. There were many disappointments, but as a generation we felt empowered, and we became empowered. Generations X, Y, Z, and beyond need to taste victory, whether large or small. Strategically, even small victories can create a sense of accomplishment that can thwart the notion that public demonstrations are great opportunities to wreak destruction throughout communities that would probably be otherwise sympathetic to the cause of those very demonstrations. In order to form a more perfect union we don't need to occupy Wall Street. In order to form a more perfect union we don't need to have a Tea Party that is nestled within one of the established two parties. In order to form a more perfect union we need to occupy local, state, and the federal governments.

Campaign Finance Reform

In order to form a more perfect union, the American people should elect representatives who are serious about campaign finance reform. The feeble attempts to reduce the influence of money on public officials and elections have spurned numerous "end arounds." For instance, the McCain-Feingold Act, which took effect in 2003, has been laughable in its purported goal of eliminating soft money from campaigns. To the horror of those committed to campaign finance reform, soft money was shifted to "527 organizations" that used the Internal Revenue Code to claim tax exemption status, and avoided having to register as political action committees (PACs). This is important because PACs are regulated by the Federal Election Campaign Act of 1971. Although it has been widely accepted that "money is the mother's milk of politics," we are long overdue for a weaning. However, with the U.S. Supreme Court decision in *Citizens United* (see Chapter 4), we are moving in the wrong direction. To correct, we should eliminate all private financing of federal campaigns for public office. Instead we should require that all candidates collect and submit signatures from 10% of the electorate. Those signatures would be verified. If candidates for public office can obtain the necessary signatures, their names are placed on the ballot, and they are entitled to equal funding and equal television access. This would broaden political participation, and give grass roots candidates the opportunity to compete on an even playing field. The funds would be provided through the same means by which matching funds are available today. The scope of this campaign finance reform would only apply to federal elections.

Economics

In order to form a more perfect union, "moral hazard" should be applied to the entire economic system, not just to Wall Street. This term has been around for centuries, and is nothing more than common sense. When a party bears little or no risk in ventures that inevitably have risk, moral hazard is present. In our economy, the financial and insurance sectors are the greatest opportunities for companies to engage in moral hazard. This would not be of such grave consequence to the American public if we would play by the rules of capitalism, but we don't. That is not to argue that the rules of capitalism are the best standard; they are just our claimed standard. For instance, under the rules of capitalism, if a company has taken undue or unwise risk, and those risks create economic failure, the company should fail. The rules dictate that market forces should be the determining factor on the success or failure of companies operating in a free enterprise system. However, that is not what occurs. While an argument that socialism is the best, or the ideal economic system is not being made here, it is puzzling why American history has several significant examples of socialist doctrine being applied in our most stressful economic times. Particularly during times of war the American government/ economy has adhered to socialist principles. But whether war torn or not, the toughest economic times in America are met with the sort of central government control of markets that would make Adam Smith proverbially roll over in his grave.

Case in point: In recent years the American government has used taxpayer dollars to bail out huge corporations that obviously made very poor business decisions. While it is a good thing for the American economy that the government bailed out major players in the American automobile manufacturing industry, the contradiction with our stated principles of free markets is more exposure of American hypocrisy. According to the principles of capitalism, which Americans blindly follow in the most stupid of ways, bankruptcy for General Motors or Chrysler was what was supposed to happen. What was not supposed to happen was dipping into the public coffers to pay for bad business decisions and practices. What is meant by the most stupid of ways is this reality: 71% of the economic activity in America is based on consumer spending. Is this a sustainable scheme? Only the stupid can think that we can maintain economic vitality while encouraging Americans to keep buying "stuff" in a society with a negative savings rate, budgetary debt in excess of $1 trillion annually, and a national debt in excess of $16 trillion. It is indeed time to pay the piper. The government bailouts have provided short term relief, but increased moral hazard by setting the precedent of nonadherence to the dictates of the free market system.

Another case in point: In recent years the financial industry has gotten away with the economic rape of the American taxpayer. In a society where the gap between the "haves" and "have nots" has exploded over the last 3 decades, our government has provided inordinate amounts of financial support for financial entities that continue to pay ridiculous executive bonuses to a gilded group of already well-to-do white males. The excuse that has been promoted by our government is that these corrupt financial institutions are "too big to fail." The reality is that these financial institutions are too powerful to regulate, which allowed them to become "too big to fail." Even more disturbing is the truth that the very same corrupt financial industry that created banks and cryptic instrumentalities of abuse has consolidated in the aftermath of the latest economic meltdown. If they were too big to fail before, what are they now? Have you ever considered the contradiction of the "trickle down theory" when juxtaposed with the reality of a shrinking middle class, stagnant wages, loss of the manufacturing sector, etc.?

No amount of quantitative easing will right our economic ship. For example, how effective can the federal reserve buying financial assets from commercial banks be if those banks don't lend the government monies that fatten their holdings? As a reminder, banks that received "too big to fail" bailout money from the government continued to pay exorbitant executive bonuses even after receiving taxpayer dollars. As a reminder, the very architects of Wall Street bailout schemes came from Wall Street (e.g., Robert Rubin, Lawrence Summers, Timothy Geithner), and will return to Wall Street after their tenure of extracting public money and sending it into the "old boy network."

A more perfect union will necessarily include an economic philosophy that is not based on individualism and greed. The elevation of the top 5% of our economic stratus to somehow possessing the values we should all emulate will continue to be a great impediment to a more perfect union. For the majority of the 20th century the top income brackets were taxed at a rate over 60%. To think that Americans are not sensible enough to tax them in excess of 40% shows the pathetic negative impact of materialism and consumerism. The credit rating of the entire nation has suffered through the protection of the segment of society that is the least vulnerable. Unemployment has risen under the trickle down theory of taxing the wealthy less, with the expectation of reinvestment into our economy. The truth is that the money the wealthy save through relatively low taxes is used to invest overseas, not here. The economic policies of this nation have transformed us from the main producer on the planet to the main consumer on the planet. The economic policies of this nation have transformed us from the #1 lender nation on the planet to the #1 debtor nation on the planet.

Electoral College

In order to form a more perfect union, the American people must eliminate the Electoral College. Sometimes it takes a circumstance as farcical as the 2000 Presidential election to expose the antidemocratic protection of elite status that is written into our Constitution. Because Americans are such poor students of history, we tend to overlook past ills, and we fail to correct them. In 1800, 1824, 1876, and 2000, the person who was sworn in as President of the United States did not win the popular vote. It is by design that the chief executive of this country that touts democracy for itself and the world is not always elected through the will of the people. It is a fact that the will of the majority of Americans who voted in November 2000 was flatly disregarded by five unelected people. The Electoral College is an antiquated institution that makes a mockery of America's brand of democracy. The only reasons why the Electoral College is tolerated is the power of the two-party system, and the difficulty the founders who created the undemocratic mechanism of elite protection built in to changing the Constitution. There have been some frustrated persons who have devised schemes to circumvent the Electoral College without amending the Constitution, but it is preferable to amend the Constitution because the process is informative and empowering for the American people. It is my position that the difficulty of changing the Constitution has the utility of building a consensus about disposing of an intolerable anachronism. Although there have been twenty-seven amendments to the Constitution, the last amendment that was meaningful to the American people was the ratification of the twenty-sixth. If the body politic can remove a tremendously unpopular mechanism of elite protection like the Electoral College, it may be possible to amend the Constitution on a more controversial topic.

Mandatory Military Service

In order to form a more perfect union the American people should support mandatory military service. The benefits of this idea are enormous. The wars in Iraq and Afghanistan are being fought by the smallest proportion of our population in our history. The burden is being disproportionately carried by those who are economically and intellectually most vulnerable. After our experience in Southeast Asia, it should have been clear to political leaders that we will not prevail in a military conflict where there is not a high degree of public support. At the outset of our current wars, there was a groundswell of support for attacking countries that had done nothing to us. Over time, the reactionaries lost face, and we are left in a quagmire. We may have gotten rid of a dictator, but it is probable that there will be continuing and increased instability in the geographical areas surrounding Iraq and Afghanistan. Political problems require political solutions, not military solutions. How many members of Congress were voting to potentially place their family members in harm's way by voting for the use-of-force resolution? I harken back to the Grantland Rice poem. The reason that World War II was the last war we won was because of the broad and sustained support for the war effort. Korea, Vietnam, Iraq, and Afghanistan have in common that the support for the war effort greatly eroded over time. In Korea there is an armistice, with no victory. In Vietnam there was a humiliating defeat. In Iraq we will have to adjust the objectives to even begin to claim victory. In Afghanistan we stand to suffer the fate of many a foolish leader over many centuries who tried to tame that backward society.

For the first two years after high school, or from the age of eighteen to twenty, all Americans should be required to join one of the branches of our Armed Forces. Freedom is not free. It is certainly understandable that some youth are legitimate pacifists, but there should be no exemptions. Conscientious objectors should be properly screened, and placed in administrative capacities. This is service to country, just as is required in places like Switzerland, Finland, Brazil, Denmark, Israel, and many other nations. There should be no consideration of gender, sexual orientation, or economic status. There should be no college deferments. The colleges and universities of this land will have more disciplined and better-grounded students because all students will have served their country.

Moreover, Americans are becoming more obese, and this has affected our youth. The reduction in unhealthy diets and lifestyles, and consequently the reduction in health care costs are also beneficial for our society. Politically, neither our political leaders, nor poorly informed Americans will be so swift to fight wars if their loved ones are potentially at risk. We will fight as a last resort, and woe be to our enemies because we would not lose another war.

Mandatory Voting

In order to form a more perfect union, the American people should demand mandatory voting. The fragility of our democracy has been exposed by the lack of choices, and by the failure of our elected representatives to follow the will of the people. However, the will of the people is not clearly expressed when huge numbers of Americans don't bother to vote. It is not as useful to debate the myriad of reasons why so many Americans don't vote as it would be to simply require them to exercise the franchise. My proposal is that voting be mandated for all those eligible if they want to enjoy the benefits of citizenship. Plainly put, if you don't vote, you don't collect Social Security payments, tax refunds, Medicare, or any other government service. The time is past when we can allow so few to decide the fate of so many. Currently, only 54% of eligible Americans vote in presidential elections. The numbers are less for midterm elections. Sometimes democracy needs assistance to be beneficial. In the democracies that have mandatory voting, the lowest turnout exceeds 80%. That is better than four out of five voters. This proposal is for a period of twenty years, because there are several examples where mandatory voting once existed, but no longer does. In those countries the voter turnout still exceeds 80%. We have to create the habit, expectation, and continuity of voting behavior in America. It is important to realize that, for the majority of American history, significant groups were not allowed to vote. The culture of voting is not very strong here when one takes into account our history, and when one reviews the voting behavior of distinct demographic slices of America. The credibility and prestige of our democracy is at risk when we live in a society where we set the worst example of all westernized countries when it comes to voting.

Presidential Terms

In order to form a more perfect union, the American people should eliminate the possibility of two elective presidential terms. This proposal would also require amending the Constitution, but it is a worthy cause. Currently, the amount of money that it takes to win the presidency has exceeded a billion dollars. The money necessary to win any number of elective offices has created the unavoidable consequence of corruption. We should change the Constitution to allow one six-year term for the president of the United States. We should eliminate a president acting, or failing to act, due to concerns about getting reelected. We should eliminate the possibility, or even the probability, that a president is motivated by concerns of offending potential political supporters. Whatever one may think of President G. W. Bush, it became abundantly clear that he took his actions out of a deep sense of personal conviction. He may have been greatly misguided, but his heart was in his decisions. In the face of risking the vitality of his own political party, he escalated the War in Iraq after the congressional midterm elections of 2006. This was because he knew he would never be up for elective office again. We need presidential leadership that does not pander to public opinion polls. Frequently, doing the right thing is doing the unpopular thing. When President Dwight Eisenhower sent the 101st Airborne troops to Little Rock Central High School to protect Black children, it was an unpopular, but righteous thing to do. At the time, President Eisenhower was serving out his second term. It is more likely that a president will do the right thing if the decision is free from concerns about the next election cycle.

Two-Party System

In order to form a more perfect union, the American people must eliminate the two-party system. The two-party system does not avail the American body politic sufficient political choices. It is quite predictable that there would be repeated stalemates and polarization with a political party system that has only two viable choices. The operative word here is viable. There are what have been deemed third parties in the United States, but the prospect of a vote for a candidate from one of those parties resulting in victory is dubious at best. Once a citizen decides to vote, she or he wants that vote to count, and to provide her or him with more than a voice. The voting citizen wants her or his vote to provide a realistic possibility of her or his choice winning the election. It is not that Americans don't vote according to their principles. It is that the culture of America is not interested in moral victories. The result is that many Americans do not vote because they do not like their choices, or they do not vote because they do not believe that their vote will make a difference, or they do vote for the lesser of two evils.

Third-party candidates have had their best success in terms of winning elective office on the local level. However, when it comes to either state-wide or national office, there is the dilution of the power of voting for a third-party candidate to a spoiler role. In 1992, approximately twenty percent of the national electorate voted for H. Ross Perot. Because of Mr. Perot's political leanings being clearly identified with the right pole of the political spectrum, he took potential votes from incumbent President G.H.W. Bush. The beneficiary was Bill Clinton, who won the presidency with a plurality. In 2000, approximately five percent of the national electorate voted for Ralph Nader. Because of Mr. Nader's political leanings being clearly identified with the left pole of the political spectrum, and also because he was an environmental candidate through the Green Party, he took potential votes from Vice President Al Gore. That five percent made the difference in the race.

In both examples, it is not the fault of the third-party candidate that the losers from the major parties did not prevail, but the third-party candidate's participation in the election was a significant factor. This is particularly true in the case of the 2000 presidential election for two reasons. First, there was no sane person who believed that Ralph Nader could win the presidency. Second, the race between the candidates of the two major parties was extremely close.

The methodology that the two major parties have used to insure their dominance over elections is control over the process of elections in this country. The two major parties also solidify their dominance over who governs through the rules that have been established in Congress. If a third-party candidate is able to get elected, she or he is faced with the choice of becoming a virtual member of one of the major parties through the caucus. The alternative is to be like a "lone wolf," which would render any third-party member politically ineffectual and inert.

The mechanism that the two major parties have used to ensure their dominance over elections is the winner-take-all system. Although this is most applicable to presidential elections, the winner-take-all system has created an undermining of the value of the one person, one vote concept. For instance, if a presidential candidate wins the popular vote in a state by the closest of margins, that candidate gets all of the Electoral College votes for that state. This is currently true in all but two states. There is a ripe argument for fundamental unfairness that exists when the voice of millions of voters can be ignored.

In order to form a more perfect union, every state in the United States should do something similar to what Maine and Nebraska do in presidential elections. Both Maine and Nebraska cast Electoral College votes based on proportional representation, as opposed to the winner-take-all system. Yet, that is only a step in the proper direction to assure true democracy in the United States. The two-party system also limits the choices in terms of who gets to participate in the political discourse through controlling public debates. But, eliminating the two-party system will not occur without changing the United States Constitution because of the previously discussed undemocratic institution known as the Electoral College.

Conclusion

In order to form a more perfect union, the American people need to consider alternative ways of thinking about our economic and political systems. Democracy and capitalism are not compatible. Democracy is not prefaced only on freedom or liberty. Democracy is also prefaced on equality. There is no equality in capitalism. There isn't even the equality of opportunity. Perhaps there was equality of opportunity when humans were living in a state of nature, but we have been living in civil societies for centuries. In civil societies there are social classes that perpetuate inequity. As long as Americans believe that we can base our socioeconomic activity on the notion that greed and material acquisition are good attributes, we are limiting the spread of democratic principles. Everyone knows that people with wealth are treated better than people who are poor. People with wealth are also treated better than any of the other economic classes. The current economic crisis has revealed the priority of protecting the interests of those who exist at the top of the socioeconomic strata. Multibillion-dollar corporations are receiving taxpayer dollars, whereas working class people are losing jobs, homes, and, in some cases, their sanity. The top 5% of income earners control 90% of the wealth in America today. Contrary to popular myth, nearly all members of the top economic class inherited their good fortune, instead of working to obtain it. Upward mobility has constricted to the point where the first generation of Americans in our history will not fare better than their parents. There are many other salient points that can be made, but in closing it is important to understand how our government functions so that we can take one of the countless approaches to political participation that will result in a more perfect union.

CHAPTER 8

For Your Consideration . . . California State Matters

1. Qualifying a proposed law in California requires _____% of the votes cast for governor in the previous election.
   - a: 50%
   - b: 5%
   - c: 15%
   - d: 25%

2. What percentage of initiatives are rejected by voters in California?
   - a: 50%
   - b: 25%
   - c: 5%
   - d: 10%
   - e: 67%

3. If it's a state executive officeholder in California, it will take (signatures on petition) _____% of those who voted in the previous state election to recall them:
   - a: 5%
   - b: 12%
   - c: 95%
   - d: 51%
   - e: 25%

4. For only the second time in U.S. history, a governor was recalled. His name:
   - a: Gray Davis
   - b: Arnold Schwarzenegger
   - c: Cruz Bustamente
   - d: Antonio Villaraigoza

5. This political group in California was responsible for weakening the party system through split ticket voting, and the elimination of the party column ballot:
   - a: the Progressives
   - b: the Doors
   - c: the Reactionaries
   - d: the Zealots

6. How does our state text describe political parties in California?

   a: they are strong
   b: they are fun
   c: they are fun and strong
   d: they are weak

7. Which California ethnic group is most underrepresented in holding public office?

   a: Hippies
   b: Asian Americans
   c: Dark Americans
   d: Light Americans

8. The voting electorate in California is more conservative because:

   a: people are closet racists out here
   b: only 81% of those age 18–24 vote
   c: people live the American Dream here
   d: only 30% of non whites vote

9. Although whites comprise only 41% of the population in California, they are _____% of the electorate.

   a: 100
   b: 50
   c: 70
   d: 25
   e: 90

10. Select a descriptive group which has the resources to collect the necessary signatures, or to pay for expensive election campaigns.

   a: broad based
   b: grass boots
   c: well-financed
   d: super duper

11. Between 1977 and 2003 the number of registered lobbyists in California:

   a: quadrupled
   b: declined
   c: doubled
   d: increased

12. According to the Census Bureau, approximately what % of "illegal" immigrants live in California?

   a: 33%
   b: 10%
   c: 25%
   d: 90%
   e: 75%

13. The biggest economic problem for minorities in California today is the cost of:

a: housing   d: drugs
b: food   e: gas
c: education

14. What is the twenty year trend of federal dollars received by California?

a: it has decreased sharply   d: it has increased slightly
b: it has increased sharply   e: it has stayed the same
c: it has decreased slightly

15. What approximate % of California is owned by the state and federal governments?

a: 50%   d: 90%
b: 10%   e: 25%
c: 100%

16. What is the number of California's delegation to the U.S. Congress?

a: 25   d: 100
b: 10   e: 55
c: 435

17. Initiative is a procedure by which voters can:

a: remove elected officials
b: propose a law or constitutional amendment
c: directly make laws
d: place candidates on a ballot

18. Grants to state and local governments designed for very specific programs and projects are referred to as:

a: block grants   d: categorical grants-in-aid
b: revenue sharing   e: porkbarrelling
c: unfunded mandates

19. This political movement introduced direct democracy to California:

a: the Workingmen's Party   d: the Rangers
b: the Progressives   e: the Grangers
c: the Toga Party

20. These immigrants provided the bulk of the cheap labor that built California's railroads:

    a: Africans
    b: Japanese
    c: Irish
    d: Mexicans
    e: Chinese

21. Which of the following cities *has not* been California's capitol?

    a: San Jose
    b: San Francisco
    c: Vallejo
    d: Benecia
    e: Sacramento

22. For every California tax dollar sent to Washington, D.C., how much is received back?

    a: 79 cents
    b: 25 cents
    c: $1.06
    d: 95 cents
    e: $1.15

23. More than _____ % of all judges, prosecutors, public defenders, and other court officials are white, even though whites are the minority in California.

    a: 80%
    b: 100%
    c: 25%
    d: 10%
    e: 50%

24. Identify the two major effects of California's "three strikes" law:

    a: the rich got richer, the poor got poorer
    b: the lamb laid down with the lion, the eagle flew
    c: quick increases in the state prison population, and in spending on prisons
    d: tort attorneys made a killing, and judges got embarrassed

25. Why did a 1999 University of California study conclude that "most of the decline in crime has nothing to do with the 'three strikes' law"?

    a: because they are Berkeley Liberals
    b: because there has not been a decline in crime
    c: because the law applies to such a small percentage of cases
    d: that wasn't the study's conclusion

26. Between the time of the beginning of the European colonization of California (1769), and the entrance into the Union (1849), what % of the native population was wiped out?

    a: 100%   d: 33%
    b: 150%   e: 67%
    c: 75%

27. How many of the 7 California State Supreme Court's current justices are Democrats?

    a: all   d: 4
    b: none   e: 1
    c: 9

28. What percentage of initiatives has passed since the beginning of the Progressive legacy (1912) in California?

    a: 50%   d: 10%
    b: 33%   e: 67%
    c: 5%

29. What percentage of California's population today do whites comprise?

    a: the majority   d: 25%
    b: 65%   e: the minority
    c: less than half

30. According to the state text, the explosion of _____ on the ballot is not due to greater democratic participation, but due to the power and opportunism of special interests.

    a: candidates   c: propositions
    b: political novices   d: third party candidates

31. The Republican failure to do this in California has resulted in Democratic majorities in the state legislature, the congressional delegation, and in all statewide offices except the governorship:

    a: register enough voters
    b: be exciting
    c: win support from minority voters
    d: be fair

32. Which California elected official held the highest national leadership position ever held by a woman?

    a: Nancy Pelosi   c: Diane Feinstein

    b: Barbara Boxer   d: Kamala Harris

33. Both the U.S. and California constitutions prohibit involuntary servitude except:

    a: for Blacks   c: to punish crime

    b: for illegal aliens   d: to pay debts

34. Do civil juries in California have to render a unanimous verdict?

    a: yes

    b: sometimes

    c: no

    d: civil juries don't render verdicts

35. Since its first passage in 1849, about how many times has the California state constitution been amended?

    a: none   d: 100

    b: 500   e: 72

    c: 27

36. According to lecture, approximately what percentage of adult people in California "make the decisions"?

    a: 150%   d: 45%

    b: 15%   e: 60%

    c: 30%

37. According to lecture, although Latinos are 32% of California's population, they are only _____% of the likely voters.

    a: 14   d: 4

    b: 7   e: 50

    c: 25

38. Since 1986, the percentage of independent voters in California has:

    a: stayed the same   c: tripled

    b: doubled   d: quadrupled

39. How many political parties qualified for the 2012 California ballot?

    a: 2   d: 12

    b: 4   e: 6

    c: 8

40. What was the basis cited by the California Supreme Court when in 2009 it ruled that same sex marriage should be again declared illegal?

    a: DOMA

    b: state law, as approved by the voters in 2008

    c: stare decisis

    d: fags are a drag

    e: dikes I don't like

41. How many of CA's 55 members of Congress are Republicans?

    a: 19   d: 25

    b: 55   e: 5

    c: none

42. Our state text (Ch. 1) detailed the "hourglass economy" due to these costs:

    a: immigration   c: prisons

    b: housing & health care   d: education

43. According to our state text (Ch. 3), although nearly 23 million Californians are eligible to vote, as few as this many actually vote:

    a: 1 million   d: 25 million

    b: 2 million   e: 8 million

    c: 20 million

44. On what basis did the U.S. Supreme Court (in June, 2013) assure the legality of same sex marriages in California?

    a: DOMA

    b: stare decisis

    c: by declaring that the defenders of Proposition 8 lacked standing

    d: by declaring all discrimination to be unconstitutional

    e: by respecting public opinion

CHAPTER 9

Table of Cases

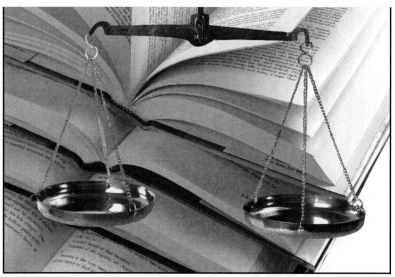

Image © JustASC, 2009. Used under license from Shutterstock, Inc.

Fisher v. University of Texas at Austin, 570 U. S. ____ (2013)

Gibbons v. Ogden, 22 U.S. 1 (1824)

Gonzales v. Raich, 545 U.S. 1 (2005)

Grutter v. Bollinger, 539 U.S. 306 (2003)

Hamdan v. Rumsfeld (Bush), 548 U.S. 557 (2006)

Hamdi v. Rumsfeld (Bush), 542 U.S. 507 (2004)

Hepting v. AT & T

Hollingsworth v. Perry, 570 U.S. ____ (2013)

Jewel v. National Security Agency, 673 F.3d 902 (Ct. App., 9th Cir., 2011)

Korematsu v. United States, 323 U.S. 214 (1944)

Loving v. Virginia, 388 U.S. 1 (1967)

Marbury v. Madison, 5 U.S. 137 (1803)

Maryland v. King, 569 U.S. ____ (2013)

McCulloch v. Maryland, 17 U.S. 316 (1819)

Miranda v. Arizona, 384 U.S. 436 (1966)

Plessy v. Ferguson, 163 U.S. 537 (1896)

Printz v. United States, 521 U.S. 898 (1997)

Rasul v. Bush, 542 U.S. 466 (2004)

Regents of the University of California v. Bakke, 438 U.S. 265 (1978)

Reynolds v. Sims, 377 U.S. 533 (1964)

Salinas v. Texas, 570 U.S. ____ (2013)

Shelby County, Alabama v. Holder, 570 U.S. ____ (2013)

Unitarian Church v. National Security Agency

United States v. Lopez, 514 U.S. 549 (1995)

United States v. Morrison, 529 U.S. 598 (2000)

United States v. Nixon, 418 U.S. 683 (1974)

United States v. Windsor, 570 U.S. ____ (2013)

Worcester v. Georgia, 31 U.S. 515 (1832)

Index

D

Declaration of Independence, 5, 16
Defense of Marriage Act (DOMA), 49–50, 80–81, 121
Democracy, 24
Democracy in America, 15
Department of Foreign Affairs, 29
Department of Homeland Security, 31, 90
Department of State, 29
Detainee Treatment Act of 2005, 89
DNA testing, 119
Dred Scott v. Sanford, 113
Due Process, 81

E

Economic Opportunity Act, 74
Economics, 144–146
Economic systems, 12–13
  capitalism, 13
  feudalism, 12
  mercantilism, 12–13
Eisenhower, Dwight D., 74, 149
Elastic Clause, 48, 117
Electoral College, 41, 85, 146–147, 150
Electronic Frontier Foundation, 71
Emancipation Proclamation, 72
English Bill of Rights, 4
English Civil Wars, 3
Enumerated powers, 47–48
Environmental Protection Agency (EPA), 30
Equal Protection Analysis, 113–114
"Era of Good Feelings," 72
Executive branch, 24, 25, 28–29
Executive Order 11905, 69
Executive Order 12036, 69

F

Fair Housing Act, 74
Family and Medical Leave Act, 80
Federal Bureaucracy, 29
Federal Bureau of Investigation (FBI), 67
Federal Circuit Courts, 33
Federal Communications Commission (FCC), 30
Federal Deposit Insurance Corporation, 73
Federal Election Campaign Act, 54
Federal Emergency Management Agency (FEMA), 30, 90
Federalist Papers, 19, 51, 23–24
Federal Reserve System, 30
Feudalism, 12
Filibuster, 26–27
Filmer, Sir Robert, 2, 3
Fisher, Abigail, 118
Fisher v. University of Texas at Austin, 118
Food Stamp Act, 74
Ford, Gerald, 69
Foreign Intelligence Surveillance Act (FISA), 70
Foreign Intelligence Surveillance Court (FISC), 70
Franken, Al, 94
Frankenstein, 79
Freedom of Information Act, 74
French and Indian War, 17
French Revolution, 3

G

Gettysburg Address, 72
Gibbons v. Ogden, 48
Gingrich, Newt, 82
Ginsburg, Douglas, 111

S

Salinas v. Texas, 120
Same sex marriage, 121
Sanders, Bernie, 27
Saudi Royal Family, 88
Second Congressional Congress, 18
Second Treatise on Government, 4
Secretary of State, 29
Select committees, 26
Seminole Wars, 72
Senate, 24, 25, 26, 41
Senate confirmation, 50–51
Senate Majority Leader, 27, 43
Senate President Pro Tempore, 28, 29
Separation of powers, 2, 4, 25
September 11, 2001, 47, 70
Sexism, 106
Shays, Daniel, 18
Shays's Rebellion, 18–19
Shelby County, Alabama v. Holder, 123–124
Shelley, Mary, 79
Simpson, O.J., 106
Slavery, 13–14, 16–17, 150
Smith, Adam, 13
The Social Contract, 4
Social Contract Tradition, 2–3
Social Security Administration, 73
Social Security reform, 87
Society of Friends (Quakers), 14
Solicitor General, 109
Sotomayor, Sonia, 50–51, 94, 108
Southern colonies, 16
Speaker of the House, 27, 43
Square Deal, 73
Stamp Act (1765), 17
Standing committees, 26
Stare decisis, 106, 114
State of the Union Address, 32

Stem Cell Research Enhancement Act of 2005, 87
Stono Rebellion, 17
Strategic Defense Initiative (SDI), 77
Strict constructionism, 116–117
Strict Scrutiny, 114, 119
Sugar Act (1764), 17
Supremacy Clause of the U.S. Constitution, 49
Supreme Court, 2, 26, 33, 45, 106–124
    5th amendment, 119–120
    affirmative action, 117–118
    Bork confirmation, 110–111
    DNA testing, 119
    equal protection, 113–114
    Fisher v. University of Texas at Austin, 118
    Hallingsworth v. Perry, 122
    inner workings of, 109–110
    judicial activism, 116
    judicial restraint, 114–115
    Maryland v. King, 119
    nomination, 108–109
Salinas v. Texas, 120
Same sex marriage, 121
Shelby County, Alabama v. Holder, 123–124
Strict constructionism, 116–117
    Thomas confirmation, 111–112
    United States v. Windsor, 121–122
    voting rights, 122–123

T

Taft, William Howard, 73
Taxation without representation, 17